College English 1

Fundamental

KMU CE1 Committee

Keimyung University Press

Contents

	Reading Texts		Vocabulary
	Main Reading	Explore Keimyung	
1. Meeting New People pp. 6 - 31	Richard Branson: Rags to Riches	- Keimyung's Own: The Success of Chang Hye-jin [KMU Core Competency: Challenging Spirit]	- Types of schools and grade levels - Common phrases used to express how you feel - Jobs, work roles, and relationships - Nouns and adjectives describing people and places - Words used to describe where you are from
2. University Life pp. 32 - 57	Those Who Volunteer	- Community Volunteering at Dongsan Medical Center [KMU Core Competency: Ethics]	- More places and things on campus - Extracurricular activities - More classes and majors - Adverbs of frequency - School activities and feelings
3. Exploring New Places pp. 58 - 83	Culture and Personal Space	- The International Lounge: A Global Hub on Campus [KMU Core Competency: Cultural Awareness]	- Words used to discuss destinations and things to do on trips - Words and phrases used to plan trips and express likes and dislikes - Things to do on a trip - Words related to booking plane tickets - Things inside an airplane
4. Planning for the Future pp. 84 - 109	What Will You Do When You Graduate?	- Career Support and Guidance at Keimyung University [KMU Core Competency: Problem Solving Ability]	- Academics - Fields of study and career fields - Careers and employment - Expressions used to show interest and understanding - Household chores

Grammar and Structures	Listening and Reading	Writing and Speaking
- Simple present *do* and *go* - *be* with *how* and adjectives; empty *it* - *be* in *wh*-questions; demonstratives; possessive adjectives - *want (to)* and would like (to) - Questions with *be like*; adjectives	L & R: Conversations about people's major and plans R: An email about the first day at work R: A travel ad L: An interview for a school newspaper R: A letter from a pen friend	W & S: Talking about jobs and requirements S: Talking about your life W: A short paragraph about your hometown S: Role-playing an interview with a famous person W: Replying to a pen friend's letter
- Prepositions of location - Gerunds - Present continuous and related time expressions - Present continuous in information questions - Simple present vs. Present continuous	R & L: A letter to freshmen R & L: Coversations about classes for your major, electives, and extracurricular activities R: A club poster R: Blank and completed questionnaires R: A description of a freshman's school life	W: Writing about places and drawing a campus map S: Talking about studying English W: A paragraph about school life W & S: Writing and talking about current activities and goals W: Filling out questionnaires and writing survey questions
- Making suggestions with *let's* + verb or *What about / How about* + verb + *-ing* - Discussing the future; showing agreement - *can* for ability; *can* and *could* for possibility - *can* for offers and volunteering; *need to* for obligation - Imperatives	R & L: Conversations about trip possibilities, preferences, plans, preparation, and booking R: Ads for travel destinations R: An email exchange about booking a trip R: A diagram of the inside of an airplane L: A conversation between a travel agent and a customer	W & S: Suggesting travel destinations W & S: Writing and talking about likes, dislikes, and future plans S: Deciding on a travel partner, where to go, and what to do W & S: Making a to-do list S: Talking to a travel agent W & S: A travel flyer W & S: Writing notes and using them to speak about adventure tours
- Present continuous for future plans - Simple present vs. Present continuous - Gerunds and infinitives; conjunction *because* - Future with *will*; *want / would like* + object + infinitive - Questions with *why* and answers; conjunction *so*	L: A radio interview R: A career flyer L & R: Conversations about options for young adults L: A conversation featuring problems and advice L: A radio announcement R: A paragraph about factors in planning for the future	W & S: Talking about plans for next month and next semester W & S: Conversations between career counselors and job seekers/ students W & S: An interview with a partner about their interests W & S: Making suggestions about what to study based on the things you know S: Talking about taking time off

Contents

	Reading Texts		Vocabulary
	Main Reading	Explore Keimyung	
5. Free Time Activities pp. 110 - 135	Walking Is Not Enough	- Tradition Meets Modern Life at Keimyung University [KMU Core Competency: Comprehensive Thinking]	- Relationships and family get-togethers - Going on a (blind) date - Types of movies and going to the movies - Going to concerts, cafés, bars, and night clubs - Weekend plans - Modals, adverbs, verb phrases, and adjective phrases used to make predictions
6. Staying Fit pp. 136 - 161	Living Right to Live Long	- Taekwondo at Keimyung University [KMU Core Competency: Adaptability]	- Sports and watching sports - Fitness and exercise - Joining a gym - Body Parts - Symptoms and illnesses
7. Healthy Eating pp. 162 - 187	Going Beyond the Familiar and Comfortable	- Keimyung's Millstones and *Doks*: Symbols of Learning and Patience [KMU Core Competency: Emotional Intelligence]	- Taking care of yourself - Eating healthily or unhealthily - Nutrition and dietary options - Shopping for food - Recipes and cooking
8. City Life pp. 188 - 213	Do Colors Make You Spend More?	- Student Culture Week at Keimyung University [KMU Core Competency: Communicative Ability]	- Shopping in the city - Taking public transportation - Shopping and trade - Buying a game - Safety information and emergency procedures

Grammar and Structures	Listening and Reading	Writing and Speaking
- Future tense - Making predictions and expressing probability with *will* and *be going to* - Modals of possibility - *that* clauses - Suggesting activities	R & L: Visiting family R: An email about a family get-together R: Online advice column R: Dating advice R & L: Going to the movie theater R & L: A night out R & L: A day trip R: A magazine article about the districts of Berlin R & L: Plans for next year	S: Your family W: A family trip W: Ideas for a blind date S: Dating advice S: Movie preferences W & S: Predictions about the future W & S: Fun things to do in your city or hometown W & S: An advertisement for a new business S: Plans for a weekend trip, including daily schedules
- Gerunds and infinitives - Suggestions and advice with gerunds, infinitives, modals, and *that* clauses - Future continuous tense - Empty *it* and *that* clauses - Present perfect vs. Simple past	R & L: Olympic sports R & L: Planning to watch a sporting event R & L: Fitness goals R & L: Fitness tips R & L: Talking about your illness and symptoms	S: Athletic dreams W & S: Favorite athletes and favorite sports to watch S: Being punctual S: Watching a sports event together W & S: A fitness plan S: Eating habits W & S: Health and fitness questionnaire S: "I have never told a lie" game
- Reported speech with infinitives; *about* for topic - Zero conditional - Reported speech with *that* clauses - Reported speech with simple present tense - First conditional	R & L: A doctor's advice L: Expert advice on nutrition R & L: A health blog R & L: Diets and eating habits R & L: Nutritional information R: Superfoods: kale and acai R: A dinner recipe R & L: Grocery shopping R: A nutritionist on cutting down on unhealthy snacks	W & S: Dietary restrictions W: Good nutrition S: Healthy and unhealthy foods W & S: Advice about eating in your country W & S: Healthy foods W & S: Suggesting a nearby restaurant S: Special foods W & S: How to cook a dish W & S: An advertisement for a food or drink S: Role-play: Making a shopping list
- Phrasal verbs - Ways to express conditions - Present perfect continuous tense - Causative verbs - Leaving out articles for brevity	R: San Francisco shopping guide R & L: Taking public transportation R & L: Shopping at the mall R & L: Buying and pre-ordering video games R: A safety poster R: Tips for tourists in New York	S: A shopping experience W: An advertisement for a local business W & S: Directions on the subway S: Propose improvements to public transportation S: Everyday technology S: Video games W: A formal email asking for a refund W & S: Safety tips, an emergency poster, and a tourist information poster W & S: Role-play: A trip to the mall W & S: Planning a trip

UNIT 1 Meeting New People

Scan and find the tracks.

Before You Read

◆ **Talk about these questions with your classmates.**

1. What makes you a successful student?
2. Who is the most successful person in your family? Why is he or she successful?
3. Who are some of the most successful people in the world?

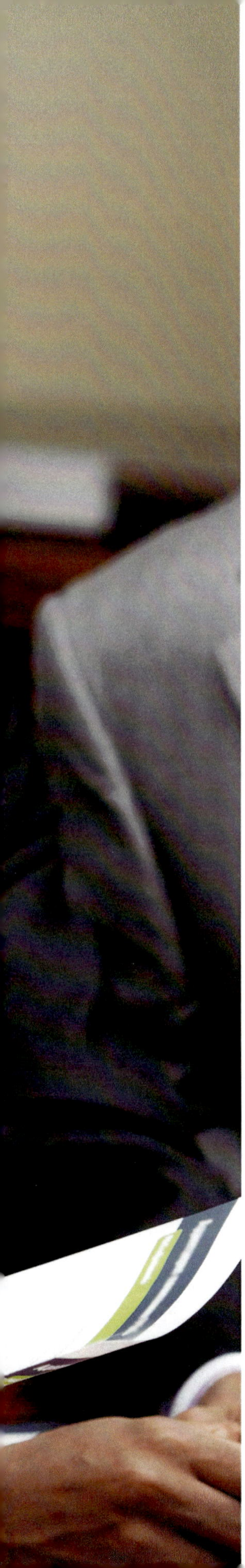

Vocabulary

◆ **Read the definitions. Then match each word in bold with its definition.**

A. something that exists or happens
B. different; not normal or common
C. when something that usually takes a long time happens very quickly or suddenly
D. to be someone's boss; to have someone working for you or your company
E. part of
F. ordinary or usual
G. to have or possess a thing
H. in important situations; being very careful or correct
I. very pleasing or appealing
J. to find something in common with someone

1. ______ Branson got **involved** in the music business when he was young.
2. ______ He is a **charming** man whom most people like immediately.
3. ______ In casual situations he is called Richard, but **formally** he is known as Sir Richard Branson.
4. ______ He got rich, and now he **owns** several companies.
5. ______ Going into space as a tourist is just a dream, but it may become a **reality** soon.
6. ______ The key to his success is his ability to **connect** with people.
7. ______ He came from **average** beginnings, but he is now worth billions of dollars!
8. ______ The magazine was so popular that it became an **overnight** success.
9. ______ His story is **unusual**, but it provides hope to people all over the world.
10. ______ In total, his companies **employ** more than fifty thousand people.

Richard Branson: Rags to Riches*

Track 001

* rags to riches: from poor to rich or unknown to well-known

Richard Branson was not a good student. In fact, he quit school at the age of 16. That, however, did not stop him from becoming successful. Today, this billionaire is formally known as Sir Richard Charles Nicholas Branson. And he is one of the richest men in the United Kingdom. He is worth about US$ 4.6 billion. He even owns his own island!

After he left school, Richard started a magazine called *Student*. It was an overnight success. From there, he got involved in the record industry. He started a successful record store in London. After that, he started a record label called Virgin Records.

Clearly, music has been important to Richard's success, but it is not the only thing he is involved in. He is the founder of the Virgin Group, which employs more than fifty thousand people and operates in fifty different countries. The group is made up of hundreds of companies. Perhaps you have flown on a Virgin Airlines plane or bought music from a Virgin Megastore. If you dream of space travel, Virgin Galactic might be able to one day make that dream a reality.

The key to Sir Richard Branson's success has been his ability to connect with people. He may not have gotten the best grades in school, but he is a charming and likeable businessman. Sir Richard's story is unusual, but it provides hope to people all over the world. From average beginnings to great success, his story is truly one of "rags to riches."

1950	Born
1966	Quit school
1966	*Student* (magazine)
1971	Record store
1973	Record label
1984	Virgin Airlines
2004	Virgin Galactic
	Present

▲ Richard Branson: a timeline

Review the Highlights

◆ **Mark up the text and infographic according to the instructions.**

1. Look at Paragraph 1. Underline how old Branson was when he left school.
2. Look at Paragraph 2. Put stars next to the ways that Branson was involved in the music industry.
3. Look at Paragraph 3. Underline the number of countries where Branson's companies operate.
4. Look at Paragraph 3. Put a star next to the name of Branson's space travel company.
5. Look at Paragraph 4. Underline what Branson's story gives to people everywhere.
6. Look at the infographic. Circle the information in the reading that goes with each event in the infographic.

Check Your Comprehension

◆ **Circle the correct answer.**

1. Which is NOT a symbol of Sir Richard Branson's success? Negative fact
   a. He owns an island.
   b. He is worth over US$ 4.6 billion.
   c. He dropped out of school.
   d. He has hundreds of companies.

2. What can be assumed about Richard Branson? Inference
   a. He knows famous musicians.
   b. He is not a nice boss to work for.
   c. He is not a very hard worker.
   d. He went to a top university.

3. What is the goal of Virgin Galactic? Details: what
   a. To make fast airplanes
   b. To make records for famous musicians
   c. To create more companies
   d. To send people into space as tourists

4. What is the reading mostly about? Main idea
   a. A person who went from average beginnings to great success
   b. A person who got successful in the UK
   c. A person who is charming and likeable
   d. A person who can make your dream a reality

5. How does Richard Branson's story provide hope to other people? Details: how
   a. They can connect with people, too.
   b. They can learn from his mistakes.
   c. They can be successful no matter how their lives start.
   d. They can copy his ideas and become rich.

◆ **Complete the summary. Write the words from the reading that best fit in the blanks. One word is extra.**

charming involved formally overnight employ connect unusual owns

Richard Branson's road to success is a(n) 1. __________ story. He quit school at a young age, but he still became successful. His first business was a magazine that became a(n) 2. __________ success. After that, he started a record store and then a record label. Many different companies followed. In fact, he 3. __________ the Virgin Group, which is made up of hundreds of companies that operate in fifty different countries. These companies 4. __________ over fifty thousand people and include music, air travel, and space travel companies. He is now 5. __________ known as Sir Richard Branson because he has become a knight. Branson's story provides hope to people all over the world. He has been so successful because he is 6. __________, and he has the ability to 7. __________ with people.

Linked Skills Activity

◆ **Richard Branson has had many different business ideas. Listen to some other people's business ideas and complete the summary.** Track 002

Sarah and Kyle have some business ideas. Kyle's idea is for 1. ______________. He wants to make it so that they can 2. ______________ lectures and make 3. ______________ for students. Sarah's first idea is for 4. ______________ on the subways. Her other idea is for an Internet 5. ______________ that has 6. ______________ twenty-four hours a day. It would be good for 7. ______________ who need help late at 8. ______________.

◆ **Work with a partner. Talk about the business ideas that you heard. Which ideas would be successful? Why? Write your reasons.**

Kyle's Idea: ______________________________

Sarah's 1st Idea: ______________________________

Sarah's 2nd Idea: ______________________________

◆ **Pretend you and your partner are going to be the founders of a business. Come up with some business ideas of your own.**

Our Ideas:

______________________ ______________________

______________________ ______________________

◆ **Discuss which idea you think would be the most successful. Once you have agreed on an idea, talk about how you might be able to make this dream a reality.**

◆ **Write a paragraph about your idea. When you are finished, use the checklist below to check your writing. Then share your idea with the rest of your classmates.**

- ☐ Did you explain your idea?
- ☐ How is your idea unusual?
- ☐ How will it be successful?
- ☐ How will you make it become a reality?

Keimyung's Own:
The Success of Chang Hye-jin

Track 003

[KMU Core Competency: Challenging Spirit]

Chang Hye-jin is a well-known archer from South Korea and a proud graduate of Keimyung University. Born in Daegu in 1987, she gained international fame after winning two gold medals at the 2016 Rio de Janeiro Olympics. She won one medal in the women's individual event and another in the women's team event. These incredible achievements made her one of South Korea's most admired athletes and highlighted how Keimyung University helps its students reach their full potential.

Her journey to success was far from easy. Chang faced many challenges and worked tirelessly to overcome them. At Keimyung University, she found the support she needed to grow and succeed. The university provided her with excellent training facilities and experienced coaches who helped her improve her athletic skills. Her professors also supported her in balancing her demanding training schedule with her academic responsibilities. This environment of encouragement and guidance helped her build a **challenging spirit**, giving her the strength to push through obstacles and aim for greatness.

Chang Hye-jin's story inspires students at Keimyung University and across South Korea. She shows that perseverance, dedication, and strong support can turn big dreams into reality. Her achievements reflect Keimyung University's commitment to student success. By sharing her story, Chang motivates others to dream big, work hard, and make a positive impact in their chosen fields. She proves that with determination and the right mindset, anything is possible.

Check Your Comprehension

1. What made Chang Hye-jin famous?
   (A) Winning a gold medal at the Tokyo Olympics
   (B) Winning two gold medals at the Rio Olympics
   (C) Becoming a coach at Keimyung University
   (D) Winning a singing competition

2. What kind of support did Chang Hye-jin receive from Keimyung University?
   (A) Financial support to travel abroad
   (B) Help with balancing her studies and training
   (C) Free accommodation for her family
   (D) A part-time job as a professor

3. What message does Chang Hye-jin's story send to students?
   (A) Success only comes with natural talent.
   (B) Working alone is better than relying on support.
   (C) Hard work, support, and determination lead to success.
   (D) Winning is more important than studying.

Talk or Write about It

1. What do you think is the most important quality for success? Why?

   ____

   ____

2. Have you ever worked hard to reach a goal? What helped you?

   ____

   ____

3. How can universities support students to achieve their goals?

   ____

   ____

1C I'm a Student

A Model Conversation

Read the conversation. Then listen. Track 004

Brief note

What are you doing? asks about your actions right now. "What do you do?" asks about your job.

Alex: Iris, let me introduce you to my cousin Kevin.
Iris: Hi, Kevin. It's nice to meet you. So, what do you do?
Kevin: I'm a college student. I start classes next week.
Iris: Oh, that's cool. I'm a student too. I attend UNM in Santa Fe. Where do you go?
Kevin: I go to Saint John's College. It's also in Santa Fe.
Iris: Aha. Alex, you're a Saint John's graduate, right?
Alex: Yeah, that's right. Class of 2009.
Iris: And how old are you, Kevin?
Kevin: I'm 18. I'm starting my first semester in college.
Iris: So you're a freshman. I remember those days. I'm a senior. I graduate next spring.
Kevin: What do you want to do after you graduate?
Iris: I'm getting a degree in computer science. I want to be a computer engineer.

B Vocabulary: The US school system

American School System—Primary and Secondary		College/University Years	
primary/elementary school	= the first years of school for children	first year	= freshman
secondary school	= middle school + high school	second year	= sophomore
middle school	= the years between primary school and high school	third year	= junior
high school	= the last years of secondary school	fourth year	= senior

Match the words from the box to the correct definitions.

1. ______ to attend
2. ______ a person working in engineering
3. ______ a way to say the year you graduated
4. ______ a title given to someone for finishing a college program (for example, BA, BS, PhD)
5. ______ a person who has a degree from a school or college program

a. go to
b. degree
c. class of…
d. engineer
e. graduate/grad

C Pronunciation

Study the pronunciations and definitions of *graduate*. Practice saying each word. Which one sounds different?

graduate[1] /græ' ɉu et/ *verb* to finish a school or college program
graduate[2] /græ' ɉu ət/ *noun* a person who has a degree from a school or college
graduate[3] /græ' ɉu ət/ *adjective* used before a noun to describe studying for a higher degree (after a BA/BS)

Write verb, noun, or adjective under the underlined words. Then listen and repeat. Track 005

1. He's a college <u>graduate</u>. 2. I'm a <u>graduate</u> student. 3. We'll <u>graduate</u> in June.

D Grammar

Simple present of *do* and *go*

Brief note

Occupation means *job* or *career*.

do	*go*
I **do**	I **go**
He / She / It **does**	He / She / It **goes**
We / You / They **do**	We / You / They **go**

Brief note

In questions like *What does he do?* and *Where does she go?* the first *do* agrees with the subject.

useful expressions		
To talk about someone's occupation (reporter' student, secretary, etc.)	A: What **does** he **do**? A: What **do** you **do**?	B: He **is** a doctor. B: I **work** for a newspaper. I **am** a reporter.
To talk about which school someone attends and what someone studies	A: Where **does** she **go**? A: What **do** you **study**?	B: She **goes** to Oklahoma State University. B: I **study** music **at** Barton College.

E Grammar Practice

Circle the correct answers.

1. What (do / are) his parents do?
2. Eleanor (does / is) an engineer.
3. My brother (works / does) at a hospital.
4. Where does Jeff (goes / go)?
5. What (do / does) they study?
6. She (goes / go) to a small college.

Fill in the blanks to complete the conversations.

7. Q: Nice to meet you. What ______ you ______?
   A: I ______ a police officer.
8. Q: What ______ your sister ______?
   A: She ______ a graduate student at Cornell.
9. Q: Which college ______ Bernard ______ to?
   A: He ______ to UCLA.
10. Q: Which medical school ______ they ______ to?
    A: They ______ to Harvard Medical School.

F Use the Language

What do they do?

Write the name of the job under each picture. (Look up any jobs you don't know.) Then talk with a partner about the jobs. What do you have to do before you can get these jobs?

______

______

______

______

______

______

______

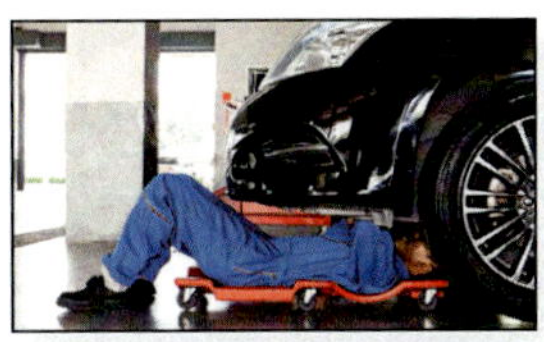
______

Check Your Progress

1 Listen to the conversation. Circle the correct answers. Track 006

1. The two men are graduates of the same (high school / university).
2. Mark is a (junior / graduate student).
3. Susan is a (junior / law school student).
4. Susan wants to be a (police officer / lawyer).
5. Dan is a (police officer / lawyer).

2 Complete the sentences with the correct forms of *do* and *go*. Then listen to the conversation again and check.

1. So, what do you ________?
2. Which university do you ________ to?
3. She wants to ________ to graduate school, too.
4. What ________ you want to study?

3 Put the words in order to make sentences.

1. does / do / what / he ______________________________?
2. wants / a / small / go / to / she / college / to ______________________________.
3. you / law school / to / which / do / go ______________________________?
4. Harvard / want / to / they / go / to ______________________________.
5. he / elementary / does / school / to / go ______________________________?

4 Match the two columns to make sentences.

1. Lauren is in her first year of •
2. Sam is taking •
3. Sonia is a graduate of this university from the •
4. Koji is getting •

• **a.** some classes at another college this semester.
• **b.** a degree in engineering.
• **c.** high school, so she is a freshman.
• **d.** class of 2015.

5 Answer the questions with information that is true for you. Then share with a partner.

1. What school do you attend? ______________________________
2. What do you study? ______________________________
3. When do you graduate? ______________________________
4. Do you like your school? Why or why not?

____

1D How Are You Doing?

A Model Conversation

Read the conversation. Then listen. Track 007

Jason: Hi. You're Wendy, right? How are you?
Wendy: I'm great, thanks. Are you the reporter from the school newspaper?
Jason: That's right. I'm Jason. Nice to meet you. Sorry I'm late. Do you still have time to talk?
Wendy: Sure. I go to work at 2:00, and it's 12:30 now.
Jason: Okay. And can we talk here, or should we go to a coffee shop?
Wendy: It's a beautiful day. Let's just sit here.
Jason: All right. I just want to ask you a few questions about the cooking contest. Congratulations on winning, by the way. So first, where do you work?
Wendy: Well, I'm a student, and I also have a part-time job as a barista.
Jason: Oh, that's surprising. The winner is usually a professional cook. How old are you, if you don't mind my asking?
Wendy: I'm 19. Cooking is my future job. I want to own a restaurant someday.

Brief note

Use the phrase "if you don't mind my asking" when you ask a personal question.

B Vocabulary

Read the conversation again. Match the expressions to the correct definitions.

1. professional
2. contest
3. win
4. newspaper
5. own
6. reporter
7. cook
8. future
9. by the way
10. congratulations

a. a person who cooks as a job or hobby
b. large pieces of paper with news and advertisements
c. a phrase used to change the topic of a conversation
d. happening at a time after now
e. doing a job that needs special education or skills
f. an event in which people try to do something better than others
g. a person who writes news, often for a newspaper
h. to be the best in a game, contest, etc.
i. to have; to possess
j. a word used to tell someone that you are happy about their good luck or success

C Vocabulary: How are you?

Study the answers to the questions "How are you?" or "How are you doing?" Then fill in the blanks.

I'm... fine sick okay well great

Worst ←-----------------------------------→ **Best**

1. tired	3. not bad	6. good / ________	7. awesome
2. ________	4. ________		8. ________
	5. ________ / all right		

Now ask two partners how they are today and tell them how you are.

D Grammar

_be_ with _how_ and adjectives; empty _it_

***be* in *how* questions**	
how + *be* + subject	How **are** you? How **is** your mother? How **am** I doing?
How far / long / much / many / old + *be* + S	How long **is** the movie? How far **is** the store? How much **is** it? How old **are** you?
adjectives after *be*	
subject + *be* + adjective	She**'s** beautiful. We**'re** awesome. I**'m** hungry.

empty *it*	
Sentences about weather, times, days, dates, and distances often have an **empty *it*** subject. It's "empty" because it doesn't replace a noun.	
weather	A: How's the weather? B: **It**'s a beautiful day. **It**'s sunny.
time	A: What time is **it**? B: **It**'s 2:00.
day/date	A: What day is **it**? / What's the date? B: **It**'s Monday. / **It**'s July 23.
distance	A: How far is **it** to campus? B: **It**'s two kilometers.

E Grammar Practice

Match the answers to the questions.

1. You're doing well.
2. It's two hours long.
3. She's great.
4. I'm 20.
5. It's okay.
6. It's $25.

a. How is your dinner?
b. How much is the pizza?
c. How old are you?
d. How long is the movie?
e. How am I reading?
f. How's your grandmother?

Write a question for each answer.

7. The theater is five miles away. How ____________________?
8. He's six feet five inches. How ____________________?
9. The show is three hours long. ____________________?
10. It's Friday. ____________________?
11. It's raining. ____________________?
12. It's March 14th. ____________________?
13. It's half past one. ____________________?

F Read to Speak

Work with a partner. Take turns reading the roles of the man and the woman in the conversation in part A. The partner playing the woman replaces the woman's information with details about his or her own life.

Present one of your conversations to the class.

Check Your Progress

1 Listen to the conversation and fill in the blanks. Track 008

Mario: Hey, Brandon! Good to see ______________. How ______________ you?

Brandon: Hi, Mario. I'm ______________. ______________ life in London?

Mario: It's good. I really like my new job there, and the city ______________ great.

Brandon: I'm glad. And ______________ your girlfriend these days? Her name ______________ Julia, right?

Mario: Right. She's fine. She's a ______________ here in town and loves it. By the way, we're getting ______________ in June.

Brandon: Really? ______________!

Mario: Thanks. Hey, ______________ are your parents?

Brandon: ______________ ______________, thanks. ______________ my dad's birthday today.

Mario: Oh, that's nice. ______________ ______________ is he now?

Brandon: Sixty years old. Actually, we're having a birthday dinner for him at 6:00. What time is ______________?

Mario: ______________ 5:35.

Brandon: Oh, I should head to the restaurant. Good ______________ you, Mario.

Mario: Good seeing you, too.

2 Put the words in order to make sentences.

1. game / this / great / basketball / is ______________________________!
2. aren't / parents / hungry / my ______________________________.
3. hard / classes / your / are / how ______________________________?
4. fine / math / is / my / class / new ______________________________.
5. far / to / is / train station / the / how / it ______________________________?

3 Match the statements with the correct pictures.

1. The food here is great! ______
2. Is your friend okay or still sick? ______
3. The weather there is usually good. ______
4. I'm well, thanks. How are you? ______

1E This Is...

A Model Conversation

Read the conversation. Then listen. Track 009

Tony: Hi, Tammy. Who's this? Oh, right. We have a new employee today. What's your name?
Tammy: Tony, this is Nick Johnson, our summer intern. Nick, this is Tony Hendricks. He's the office secretary.
Nick: Nice to meet you, Tony.
Tony: Welcome to the company.
Tammy: Here Nick, have a seat. This is Elaine Rodriguez, and that's our supervisor, Stacy Ramon.
Nick: Nice to meet both of you.
Stacy: Glad to meet you too. How's your first day going?
Nick: I like my coworkers, but I'm still finding my way around.
Stacy: Well, you have lots of time. After the meeting, let's go and see Mr. Carlson.
Nick: Okay. Um, who is Mr. Carlson?
Stacy: He's our boss, the CEO.

Brief note

"Have a seat" is a polite way of asking someone to sit down.

Brief note

"Supervisor" is another word for *boss* (see part B). It is usually used for a lower boss who works closely with employees, not a CEO.

B Vocabulary

Read the conversation again. Match the expressions to the correct definitions.

1. coworker	**a.** a business
2. company	**b.** chief executive officer; the boss of a company
3. intern	**c.** a person whose job is to answer phones, etc.
4. employee	**d.** a person who works at a job for a short time to learn about it
5. CEO	**e.** a person whose job is to tell others what to do
6. secretary	**f.** a time at work when people get together to discuss something
7. boss	**g.** a person who works for another person or for a company
8. meeting	**h.** a person you work with

C Vocabulary Comprehension

Read Nick's email to his parents about his first day at work. Circle the correct answers.

Hi, Mom and Dad.

My first day at the 1 (company / employee) is going fine. I don't have a computer yet, so I'm borrowing a tablet from the 2 (meeting / secretary). His name is Tony. A 3 (secretary / coworker) named Tammy introduced me to the other 4 (companies / employees) in the office. She seems very nice. So does Stacy, my 5 (intern / supervisor).

We just had a 6 (boss / meeting) about this week's work. Soon Stacy is taking me to meet the big 7 (boss / employee)—the CEO! I'm a little nervous. More later.

Love,
Nick

D Grammar

be in *wh-* questions; demonstratives; possessive adjectives

be in *wh-* questions
***Wh-* word + *be* + S (+ more information)**
Where am I right now, and **where am** I going? **What are** you guys studying? **Who is** that woman? **When are** those meetings? **Why is** this so hard?

Brief note

Remember, demonstratives (*this*, *that*, *these*, and *those*) can come before a noun, or they can be alone.

possessive adjectives	
singular	**plural**
my coworker **your** office **his** parents **her** brothers **its** CEO	**our** boss **your** company **their** supervisor

Brief note

Possessives say who has something.

- You can also use a noun to talk about who has something. Add *-'s* to a singular noun or *-s'* to a plural one: *Erik's potatoes* (one person has potatoes); *the boys' room* (many boys live in a room).
- Use the question word *whose* to ask about who has something: *Whose dog is that?*

E Grammar Practice

Circle the correct answers.

1. What's (your / our) name?
2. (Who's / Whose) phone is this?
3. (Where / Here) do you live?
4. (When / Who) is your daughter's birthday?
5. The students have (there / their) pencils.
6. Is (this / these) the (boy's / boys') bathroom?
7. I enjoyed meeting (my / mine) new coworkers yesterday.
8. (This / These) math problems are more difficult than (this / those) problems.
9. (This / That) book in my hand costs more than (this / that) one over there.
10. (Where / What) is the name of (your / your's) family's company?
11. (Whose / Who) is your boss? (When / What) time is he arriving?
12. (Marks' / Mark's) keys aren't here. (Where / When) are they?

F Write to Speak

Find a partner. Ask questions about your partner and write the answers.

____

____

____

____

____

G Use the Language

This is my partner...

Find another pair. Introduce your partner to them. Then walk around the room and introduce your partner to at least three other pairs.

Check Your Progress

1 Complete the crossword.

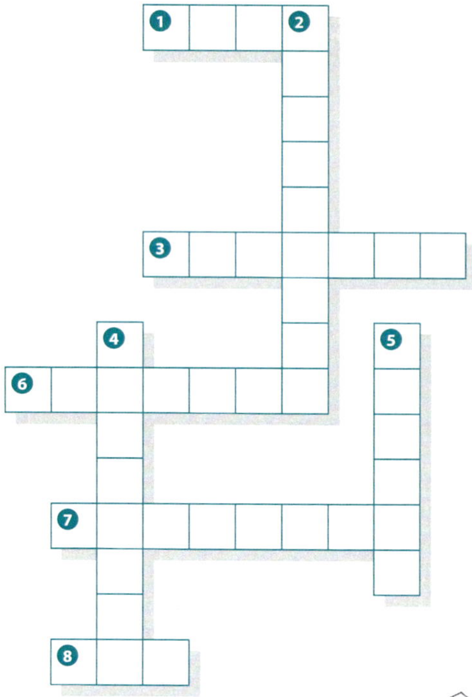

Across →

1. a person who tells employees what to do
3. The ______ is at 4:30 in room 214. See you there!
6. He's our boss. He owns the ______.
7. a person you work with
8. chief executive officer

Down ↓

2. a person whose job is to answer phones, etc.
4. a person who works for another person
5. Our ____ is a college student. She's learning about the business.

2 Read the email. Circle the correct answers.

NEW MESSAGE
To: Lauren@jmail.com
Subject: Hello!

Dear Lauren,

How ❶ (are / is) you? I have some news.
Our new intern is Edward Smith. I think he's a good choice for ❷ (this / that) company.

Edward is very nice. And ❸ (his / he) university program is very good. ❹ (Edwards / Edward's) professors say he has good grades. I think he's a good employee. I hope you agree with ❺ (my / your) opinion.

Please call Edward and ask him to come here tomorrow morning. He can use ❻ (Peter's / Peters') old office. ❼ (That / Those) office is empty now.

By the way, ❽ (when / where) is our next meeting? Is it on Wednesday or Thursday?

Thanks,
John

3 Listen to the conversations and put a check mark (✓) next to the correct use of the apostrophe ('). Track 010

Brief note

An *apostrophe* is the ' before the *-s* in phrases like *Mark's car*.

Conversation 1: Whose party?
☐ her boyfriend's party ☐ her boyfriends' party

Conversation 2: Whose new supervisor?
☐ Michelle's new supervisor ☐ Michelles' new supervisor

Conversation 3: Whose dog?
☐ his parent's dog ☐ his parents' dog

1F Jobs

A Model Conversation

Read the conversation. Then listen. Track 011

Brief note

Use *This is...* to introduce someone informally. In more formal conversations (with a boss, professor, etc.), people often use these phrases:
I'd like to introduce you to...
I'd like you to meet...
Let me introduce...

Teacher: Sonia, I'd like to introduce you to Mr. Peters. He's our **career counselor**. Mr. Peters, this is Sonia. She wants some **advice**. She's choosing her classes for next **semester**.

Mr. Peters: Hi, Sonia. So what do you want to do after you graduate?

Sonia: Well, I'd like to be a pop star, but I can't sing. Anyway, I like clothes, and I love drawing. Maybe I want to be a fashion designer. Of course, I also like money. Maybe I want to be a CEO.

Mr. Peters: So art, design, and business could be good classes for you. Let's look at the schedule.

Brief note

Pop, as in *pop music* or *pop star*, is short for *popular*. Something popular is something a lot of people like.

B Vocabulary

Match the words to the correct definitions.

a. graduate	_____ having many new ideas
b. draw	_____ a popular singer
c. pop star	_____ a person who makes clothes
d. clothes	_____ things to wear
e. creative	_____ to finish school or college
f. fashion designer	_____ to make a picture

Look back at the conversation in part A. Write the bold words next to the correct definitions.

1. ____________________ an opinion told to someone about what he or she should do

2. ____________________ a job that someone does for a long time; a person's work life

3. ____________________ a person whose job is to listen and give advice

4. ____________________ half of a school or university year, often eighteen weeks

C In Your World

Fill in the blanks. Then read your answers to your classmates and listen to their answers.

I want to take a(n) ____________________ class. I want to be a(n) ____________________.

D Grammar

want (to) and *would like (to)*

Brief note

Sometimes *want* and *would like* can be used in the same place. At those times, *would like* is more formal than *want*.

want / would like + noun	*want to / would like to* + verb
Would like + noun is a less direct, more polite way of saying that you want something.	*Would like to* means *want to*. It is less direct, so it can also be used for wishes that cannot happen.
I **want** a pizza. / I **would like** a pizza. I **want** some new clothes. / I **would like** some new clothes.	I **want to** become a fashion designer. I **would like** to become a fashion designer. I **would like** to be a pop star (but I can't sing).
To make short forms with *would like*, add *-'d* to the subject pronoun: *I'd, you'd, he'd, she'd, it'd, we'd, they'd.* I'**d like** to see a career counselor. She'**d like** dessert. We'**d like** to graduate this year.	

E Grammar Practice

Put the words in order to make sentences.

1. like / you / would / or / coffee / tea

   ______________________________?

2. lawyer / a / be / to / like / he'd

   ______________________________.

3. do / you / what / like / would / to

   ______________________________?

4. class / want / a / business / they / good

   ______________________________.

5. go / like / moon / to / I'd / the / to

   ______________________________.

F Listen to Speak

Read the information. Then listen to the introductions. Write the name of the person in each blank. Track 012

He's married and has a son. He loves his job and likes to give advice to students. In the summer, he travels with his family. He'd like to go to Mt. Everest, but he's too busy. __________	She's married, with no kids. She studies computer science in college and also works at a big company. She wants to be a CEO someday. __________	She's single and lives with her best friend. They're creative and love the arts. She's a part-time barista now, but she would like to be a movie star. __________

1. Interview a partner about a person he or she knows (not a classmate).
2. Tell your classmates about the person, and answer any questions they have.

Check Your Progress

1 Fill in the blanks with the correct verbs to complete the sentences.

want	play	be	study	like	would

1. Do you want to ____________ a famous pop star or movie star?
2. I ____________ like some salad, please.
3. She's creative, and she'd like to ____________ art.
4. My parents ____________ to meet my new boyfriend.
5. I'd ____________ to talk to my career counselor, Cynthia.
6. The guys next door want to ____________ video games with us.

2 Gurdeep, Hillary, and Sammy are having a conversation. Put the following sentences in the correct order.

____ Hello, Sammy. I work with Gurdeep here at the school. I'm his supervisor.

____ I'm great. I'd like to introduce you to my cousin Sammy, from Australia. Sammy, this is Hillary.

____ Oh, Sammy is a great teacher. He's better than me.

____ Hi, Hillary. How are you?

__1__ Oh really? I'd like to hear about your school and your work down there, Sammy.

____ Nice to meet you, Hillary.

____ Hey, Gurdeep. I'm doing well, thanks. And you?

____ I know. Actually, I'd like to ask you for some advice. I want to find a teaching job here. I'm a teacher in Australia.

3 Read the conversations and match them to the pictures. Then listen and check. Track 013

A: I'd like to meet new people. What's your advice?
B: Let's get together on Saturday. I want to introduce you to my friends from school.

____

A: Marcia, I'd like to introduce you to Peter Snell. Mr. Snell is our CEO.
B: Nice to meet you, Mr. Snell. I'm Marcia, the new designer.

____

A: Hey, you're in our drawing class, right? Do you want to sit down and join us?
B: Sure.
A: Cool. What's your name?

____

1G From Where?

Brief note

To ask about someone's hometown, say, "Where are you from?" The answer is, "I'm from..."

A Model Monologues

Read the monologues. Write the number of each monologue next to the correct picture. Then listen. Track 014

1. **Man:** I'm from San Francisco. It's an urban area in the state of California. There's a very famous bridge there; the Golden Gate Bridge. San Francisco is beside a bay. There are tall buildings, and some mountains are nearby. I love my hometown.

2. **Woman:** I'm from Helena, Montana. It's small, but it's a beautiful town. It's very rural. It usually snows a lot in the winter, but the summer is very hot. It's an awesome place.

3. **Man:** My hometown is Nashville, Tennessee. People call it "Music City." You can hear all kinds of music every night, but country music is the most popular. Nashville is also famous for great food, and the people are really nice.

Brief note

Rural areas are often called *the country*. *Country music* is a kind of music about the lives of people in the country.

B Vocabulary

Match the words to the correct definitions.

1. famous •	• very pretty
2. hometown •	• a part of a larger place
3. beautiful •	• known to very many people
4. area •	• the city or town where a person is from
5. state •	• a part of a country that can make some of its own laws.

C In Your World

Use a dictionary. Find five English adjectives that describe your hometown. Write them here.

1. ____________ **2.** ____________ **3.** ____________ **4.** ____________ **5.** ____________

D Grammar

Questions with *be like*; adjectives

Brief note

Go back to p. 11 to review S + *be* + adj. See p. 73 to learn about adjectives after other verbs.

questions with *be like*	adjectives	
These questions ask you to describe a person or place.	You can describe things using adjectives. Adjectives can come after some verbs or before nouns.	
***What* + *be* + S + *like* (+ more information)?**	**S + V + adj.**	**(article +) adj. + N**
What **is** he **like**? What**'s** Paris **like** at night? Who's your favorite professor? What**'s** she **like**? What **are** your parents **like** when they're angry?	He's **calm** and **quiet**. It's **beautiful** and **exciting**. She's **loud** and **passionate**.	a **quiet** man **beautiful** lights She's a **passionate** person.

E Grammar Practice

Brief note

Remember to use *a* before words that begin with a consonant sound and *an* before words that begin with a vowel sound.

Put the words in order to make sentences.

1. mother / is / what / your / like ______________________________?
2. your / like / siblings / are / what ______________________________?
3. blue / Marcia / a / has / car ______________________________.
4. in / house / an / boy / lives / tall / the / old ______________________________.
5. beautiful / famous / she's / and ______________________________.

F Read to Write

Read the advertisement. Underline the adjectives. Look up any words you don't know.

G Use the Language

Traveling to my hometown

What's your hometown like? Why would travelers like to go there? Write a paragraph about it. Look back at part C for ideas.

My hometown: ______________

Check Your Progress

1 **Underline the errors and rewrite the sentences correctly. For correct sentences, write *correct*.**

1. What Rebecca is like?

   ____

2. What's the food like in your country?

   ____

3. Her rural area is in a hometown.

   ____

4. The mountains in my hometown are beautiful.

   ____

5. John wants to be a singer famous.

   ____

2 **Match the questions and answers.**

1. Where are you from? •
2. Where's the Golden Gate Bridge? •
3. What's the traffic like in an urban area? •
4. What is the weather like near the bay? •
5. What's Samantha like? •

- • **a.** It's hot and rainy there.
- • **b.** I'm from Munich, Germany.
- • **c.** She's quiet, and she's a good student.
- • **d.** It's in San Francisco, California.
- • **e.** It's crowded and slow.

3 **Fill in the blanks with *a* or *an*.**

1. ______ country **2.** ______ rural area **3.** ______ older car **4.** ______ bridge **5.** ______ apartment

4 **You are meeting someone for the first time. That person asks you some questions about your life. Write your answers below.**

1. Where are you from? ______________________________.
2. What's the weather like in your hometown? ______________________________.
3. What's the food like there? ______________________________.
4. What are the people like there? ______________________________.
5. What is a famous place there? ______________________________.
6. What is your family like? ______________________________.

Unit Review

A An Interview

Listen to a conversation between a reporter for the school newspaper and a college soccer player. Fill in the blanks with the words that you hear. Track 015

Jamie: Excuse me. ______________ you Daniel Bell?

Daniel: Yes, I ______________. Hello. Are you the reporter?

Jamie: Yes. Jamie White, from the university newspaper. Nice to ______________ you.

Daniel: Nice to meet you, too. Have a ______________.

Jamie: Thanks. By the ______________, congratulations on ______________ the big game!

Daniel: Thanks. Yeah, it feels good to win.

Jamie: In the story, I'm going to ______________ you to our readers. So first, ______________ are you from?

Daniel: A small town in the ______________ of Washington, near Seattle.

Jamie: How ______________ life there?

Daniel: ______________. It's a beautiful area.

Jamie: ______________ your family there?

Daniel: Yes, they ______________. I have two brothers there. They love soccer, too.

Jamie: So, what about your career, if you don't ______________ my asking? Would you like to be a ______________ soccer player?

Daniel: No, actually. I want to be a ______________, like you.

B Interview a Famous Person

With a partner, think of a famous person that you both know a lot about. Use the Internet for ideas. Then decide on roles. One of you is that person, and the other is a reporter interviewing him or her. Role-play the interview. Try to include the following:

- Introductions
- Where the person is from
- Basic details about the person's family and career
- What the person wants to do in the future

Further Practice

A Read to Write

Read the letter from your new pen friend.

Hello,

How are you? Let me introduce myself. My name is Anaya, and I live in Vancouver, Canada. I'm 20 years old, and I go to the University of Art and Design. The campus is beautiful. I like urban life! It's new for me because I'm from a rural area in India. My parents and my brother live there.

I study web design, the designing of websites. I'm creative, and I love computers. Someday, I'd like to own a web design company. My classes are hard, but I like them. I study a lot, but I also have fun with my friends. Vancouver is amazing.

What about you? Are you a student? What's your hometown like? What's your future career? Is your family big? Sorry—that's a lot of questions! By the way, I'm sending a photo. Can you please send me one, too?

Anaya

B Prewrite

Get ready to write to Anaya. Use the letter to fill in Anaya's answers to the questions, and then fill in your answers. Think of two more questions you'd like to ask her.

	Anaya	You
How old are you?		
Where are you from?		
What are you like?		
What's your future career?		

C Now Write

Respond to Anaya's letter. Introduce yourself, answer her questions, and ask your questions. Start here and, if necessary, continue on a separate piece of paper.

MEMO

UNIT 2

University Life

Scan and find the tracks.

Before You Read

◆ **Talk about these questions with your classmates.**

1. Have you ever given money to a charity? If so, which charity was it?
2. How can people help charities, other than by giving money to them?
3. Why might it be better for a charity to get something other than money?

Vocabulary

◆ **Read the definitions. Then match each word in bold with its definition.**

A. a person who is under the care of a doctor
B. needing or requiring care or help
C. to give out; to hand out
D. an organization that works to help people who are in need
E. to give (money, clothes, food, time, etc.) for free in order to help others
F. a piece of paper that proves a person finished college or university
G. a special ability that allows someone to do something well
H. to offer to do something without being asked or required

1. _____ How many volunteer hours per year are spent treating **needy** patients?
2. _____ Doctors **donate** many different talents, not just their medical talents.
3. _____ Everyone has a **talent** that they can share with other people.
4. _____ Surveys show that people are more likely to **volunteer** if they are educated.
5. _____ Some **patients** are helped or treated by volunteers.
6. _____ Volunteer workers often serve food or **distribute** clothing to those in need.
7. _____ Volunteers in the US tend to be women who have college **degrees**.
8. _____ Many doctors do **charity** work.

2A Main Reading

Those Who Volunteer

Track 016

Everyone has some talent to share as a volunteer. The problem is that many people do not recognize their talents. So what kinds of people usually do volunteer work? Surveys show that the more education a person has, the more likely he or she is to volunteer. Consider doctors. They spend more years studying than just about anybody. Do doctors do a lot of volunteer work? Yes. In fact, medical doctors are a lot more likely to volunteer than other people.

Surprisingly, not all of those medical doctors treat patients when they volunteer. On average, only three percent of all volunteer hours per year are spent treating needy patients. Doctors, like other people, donate many different talents besides their medical talents. Most often, volunteer workers serve food or distribute clothing to those in need. About fifteen percent of volunteer hours each year are spent on these activities. Other common charitable activities include teaching and physical work, such as building things.

Does this mean that most volunteers who serve food are doctors? No, it doesn't. There are a little under one million doctors in the US. Of that number, two-thirds volunteer to do charity work. But millions of people in the US volunteer to do charity work each year. Most of the volunteers are women. Of those women, the majority are between 35 and 45 years old. They typically also have college degrees of some kind. In addition, they are very likely to be married and to have children.

▲ Women volunteer more often than men.

Education level

Volunteer activities

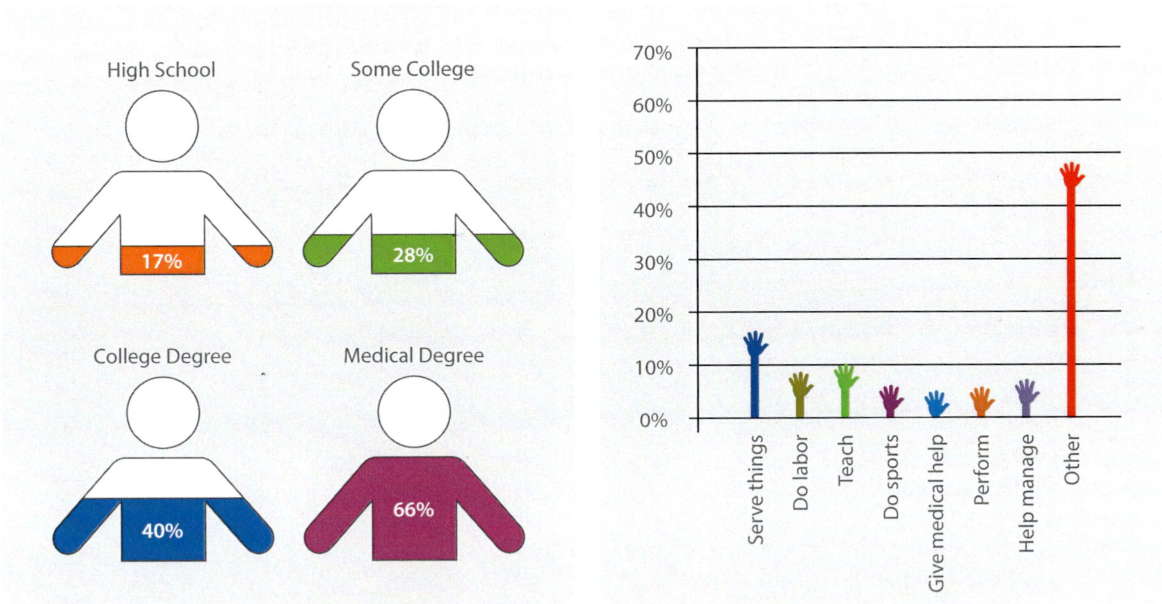

▲ Percentage of volunteers by educational level and the volunteer work they do

Review the Highlights

◆ **Mark up the text and infographic according to the instructions.**

1. Look at Paragraph 1. Underline the key characteristic of volunteers mentioned.
2. Look at Paragraph 2. Underline the information that contrasts with the idea at the end of Paragraph 1.
3. Look at Paragraph 2. Circle the two most common types of volunteer activity.
4. Look at Paragraph 3. Circle the four characteristics of volunteer women mentioned.
5. Look at the infographic. What information do both parts of the graphic show?

   Check your choice: ☐ Organizations ☐ Percentage of volunteers ☐ Types of talents

Check Your Comprehension

◆ Circle the correct answer.

1. What is the reading about? Main idea
   a. A charity organization b. Needy patients
   c. Volunteer doctors d. People donating talents

2. To which group of people do most volunteers belong? Details: who
   a. Colleges b. Doctors c. Teachers d. Women

3. What information is the focus of the infographic? Purpose
   a. Doctors and patients b. Organizations and schools
   c. People and activities d. The poor and the needy

4. Which volunteer activity is NOT mentioned in the reading? Negative fact
   a. Watching children b. Distributing clothing
   c. Treating patients d. Building things

5. What can be inferred from the information in the reading? Inference
   a. More than half a million doctors in the US do volunteer work.
   b. Most of the women who volunteer have jobs as doctors.
   c. The food served to the needy is quite easy to prepare.
   d. Women who have children do not have time to work with charities.

◆ Complete the summary. Write the words from the reading that best fit in the blanks. One word is extra.

charities distribute donate degrees needy patients talent volunteer

People with more schooling tend to 1. ______________ more often. In fact, the majority of people with medical 2. ______________, who usually have the most years of schooling, volunteer with 3. ______________. Many of these doctors do not 4. ______________ their medical talent to help needy 5. ______________. Instead, they serve food or 6. ______________ clothing when they volunteer. These doctors give their time to help 7. ______________ people as they work beside other volunteers.

Linked Skills Activity

◆ **Look at the following information about three volunteers. Then list two volunteer activities that each person would do well. Compare your ideas with a partner.**

Name: Brian Smith Age: 32 Job: music teacher Hobbies: video games, painting	Name: Anna Walker Age: 18 Job: student Hobbies: hiking, soccer	Name: Carol Richards Age: 44 Job: dentist Hobbies: gardening, blogging

◆ **Read the following information about four charity organizations. Choose one organization for each person above to work with. Then compare your choices with your partner.**

PROJECTS ABROAD

This organization matches volunteers with a range of projects worldwide. They accept volunteers between the ages of 16 to 75. Volunteer opportunities include a variety of projects from building to sports to medicine.

GLOBAL VOLUNTEERS

This volunteer vacations organization was founded in 1984. It finds opportunities for a variety of short-term volunteer projects overseas. Volunteer opportunities include projects for the benefit of children and youth.

WWOOF

World Wide Opportunities on Organic Farms, or WWOOF, is an organization that matches volunteers with organic farms worldwide. In return for volunteer work, farms provide food and housing.

GLOBAL CITIZEN YEAR

This program places high school seniors in projects in needy regions. Global Citizen Year's mission is to provide young people with experience and tools for future success. There are various projects in regions such as Brazil, Ecuador, and Senegal.

Anna Walker → ____________________

Brian Smith → ____________________

Carol Richards → ____________________

◆ **Choose one of the topics below. Discuss them with a partner.**

1. Are you more interested in volunteering locally or abroad? Why?
2. Which of your hobbies and talents would benefit a charity organization?

Community Volunteering at Dongsan Medical Center

Track 017

[**KMU Core Competency:** Ethics]

In 2020, Keimyung University's Dongsan Medical Center became a symbol of hope and responsibility during one of the most challenging times in recent history. As COVID-19 spread across Korea, the hospital focused on treating infectious diseases by relocating non-COVID patients to other facilities. This decision showed Dongsan's commitment to healthcare, kindness, and Christian values, even in difficult circumstances.

Supported by over 100 doctors and nurses from nearby hospitals, the Dongsan team worked tirelessly to care for more than 260 patients during the peak of the pandemic. Their teamwork and sacrifice not only saved lives but also helped Daegu become a "K-Quarantine" model city, showing how **ethics** and organized healthcare can protect communities during emergencies.

Volunteers, including Keimyung students, played a vital role by supporting staff and assisting patients in various ways. Their actions reflected a deep sense of responsibility and ethical behavior; values strongly emphasized at Keimyung University.

Dongsan Medical Center's mission—being a leader in treatment, education, and research—guided its work throughout the pandemic. To honor these efforts, the hospital created a special "COVID-19 Memory Space." This space recognizes the selflessness of staff and volunteers and the ethical values that inspired them to act during a crisis.

By stepping up during such a difficult time, everyone at Dongsan Medical Center added to its proud history of care and innovation. Their actions continue to inspire others to serve with compassion, determination, and ethics.

Check Your Comprehension

1. What did Dongsan Medical Center do during COVID-19?
   (A) Became a school
   (B) Treated COVID-19 patients
   (C) Built new homes
   (D) Stopped working

2. How many COVID-19 patients did the hospital care for during the peak of the pandemic?
   (A) Over 50
   (B) Over 100
   (C) Over 260
   (D) Over 500

3. Why does the hospital have a "COVID-19 Memory Space"?
   (A) To honor the people who worked hard
   (B) To show new medical tools
   (C) To celebrate a new building
   (D) To thank COVID-19 patients

Talk or Write about It

1. What kind of volunteer work have you done before?

   ____

   ____

2. What are some ways students can help their community?

   ____

   ____

3. Why do you think talent donation is important for a community?

   ____

   ____

2C Where Is It?

A Authentic Text: A letter to freshmen

Read the letter. Then listen. Track 018

Welcome, freshmen!

We want to introduce you to the campus and help you learn where some things are.

One of the first things you see when you come into the front entrance is the large fountain in the middle of the south courtyard. Behind that is the admissions office. The science library is on the left, and on the right, next to the admissions office, is the administration building. The academic center, the housing office, and many other offices are inside.

There are two main paths out of the courtyard. The path between the science library and the admissions office takes you toward our athletic center and the food court. The wide path on the right, past the administration building, leads to the dormitories and the middle of campus. Around there are the academic buildings, where most classrooms are located.

Visit our information center to learn more about your new campus!

Brief note

Something "academic" is related to school and studying.

B Vocabulary: Around campus

Common Campus Locations			
laboratory (*or* lab)	student center	administration building	academic center
housing office	financial aid center	athletic center	food court
concert hall	garage	auditorium	courtyard

C Vocabulary Comprehension

Look back at part B. Where can you find the following things? Discuss with a partner.

1. a place to exercise and play sports
2. music performances
3. help getting a place to live
4. an open area with buildings around it
5. information about clubs and social activities
6. parked cars
7. help with money to pay for college
8. offices of the president and college employees
9. places to eat
10. shows and speeches
11. science projects
12. tutors and counselors to give advice on classes

D In Your World

Write one to three sentences about a place that you often go, such as your school. Where is it? What kind of transportation do you use to get there? Share your sentences with a partner.

E Grammar

Prepositions of location

prepositions	examples
next to / beside	The library is **next to** the athletic center.
near	There is an information center **near** the dormitory.
in front of	Let's meet **in front of** the food court
behind	Do you know what's **behind** the auditorium?
around	There are a lot of buildings **around** the courtyard.
inside	The academic center is **inside** the administration building.
outside	A beautiful garden is **outside** my dormitory.
between ____ and ____	The fountain is **between** the admissions office **and** the courtyard.
on the right / left of	**On the left of** the housing office, you can find the president's office.
across ____ from / opposite	My office is **across** the hall **from** the financial aid center.

Brief note

We can say *across from...* or put a noun between those words in phrases like *across the street from...*

F Grammar Practice

Circle the correct answers.

1. The nose is (next to / between) the eyes.
2. The dormitories are (between / around) the courtyard.
3. The auditorium is (opposite / across) the street from the post office.
4. Can you please move? I can't see what's (behind / around) you.
5. You live (on the right of / near) the bus stop, so you really don't need a car.
6. Why are these books (inside / outside) the library? They should be (inside / outside) on the shelves.

Put the words in order to make sentences.

7. sit / to / next / down / me / please ________________________________.
8. the / I / school / my / from / across / live / street ________________________________.

G Use the Language

A campus and its surroundings

Ask your partner to describe the buildings and places on a college campus. Draw a simple map of the campus your partner describes. Then ask about some things that are around the outside of the campus and draw them.

Now show your map to your partner. Is it right?

Check Your Progress

1 Listen to the conversation. Circle true or false. Track 019

1. Anna needs to find the financial aid center. true false
2. Josh wants to go to the library to get some books. true false
3. The library is on the left side of the path. true false

2 Listen again and fill in the blanks.

Anna: Hi, Josh. You look lost. Can I ______ ______ find something on campus?

Josh: Yes, please. I'm trying to get to the ______ ______ center. Then after that, I'm meeting my friends for lunch at the ______ ______.

Anna: Okay. Well, the financial aid center is ______ the library and the athletic center.

Josh: Oh, I should stop by the ______ to get some books, too. How do I get there from here?

Anna: Just walk along this path. It's on the ______.

3 Put the words in order to make sentences. (Answers may vary.)

1. campus / I / find / can't / way / around / my

______.

2. in front / the / admissions office / of / the / courtyard / is

______.

3. right / the / on / are / dormitories / the

______.

4. the / located / inside / housing office / administration building / the / is

______.

4 Look at the map. Circle the correct answers.

1. The courtyard is (between / in front of) the admissions office and the dormitories.
2. The library is (inside / behind) the admissions office.
3. The housing office is (next to / around) the dormitories.

2D I Love Doing Experiments

A Model Conversation

Read the conversation. Then listen. Track 020

Yolanda: What's your major?

Pete: I'm studying Russian language and literature.

Yolanda: Wow. How's that?

Pete: Well, reading Russian is a lot of fun. I understand it pretty well when I go slowly. But listening is really difficult for me.

Yolanda: Oh yeah? When I study foreign languages, reading is more difficult.

Pete: Not for me. Understanding a fast talker is hard. Anyway, what's your major?

Yolanda: I'm studying physics.

Pete: Oh, cool. What do you like about it?

Yolanda: I love doing experiments in the lab and research in the library. But I hate the lectures. They're boring. My professor talks too much.

Brief note

A "lecture" is an academic talk. In a lecture, the teacher speaks and the students listen.

B Vocabulary: Activities and feelings

solving problems	doing experiments	taking notes	doing research
*I **like** solving math problems.* *like* = have a good feeling about	*I **love** doing science experiments.* *love* = a stronger feeling than *like*	*I **dislike** taking notes in class.* *dislike* = the opposite of *like*	*I **hate** doing research in the library.* *hate* = a stronger feeling than *dislike*

Brief note

It's more common to say *don't like* than *dislike*.

Fill in the blanks with the correct forms of the verbs. (Answers may vary.)

1. My chemistry class is great. I love ____________ ____________ in the laboratory.
2. I'm good at writing, but I ____________ ____________ notes in class. It's just not very fun for me.
3. Cassandra really ____________ ____________ mathematics problems. I asked her to help me with my math homework, and she got angry!
4. David is doing ____________ for a history report. He doesn't ____________ it, but he says it's not too bad.

C In Your World

Talk to a partner about learning English. Talk about listening, speaking, reading, and writing.

Which is easy for you, and which is hard? Which is most important? Why?

What are some good ways to learn each of the language skills?

D Grammar

Gerunds

gerunds	
A gerund looks like a verb with an *-ing* ending, but it is used like a noun. It can be a subject, or it can be the object of verbs such as *like* or *avoid*.	
gerunds as subjects	**gerunds as objects**
Swimming is fun. **Reading** bores me. **Watching** horror movies scares me. ← **Brief note** The subject here is *watching*, and it is singular even though *horror movies* is plural.	I like **swimming**. I don't enjoy **reading**. I avoid **watching** horror movies.

some verbs with gerunds as objects				
like	dislike	avoid	consider	continue
love	enjoy	stop	start	practice
hate	prefer	quit	keep	imagine

E Grammar Practice

Put the words in order to make sentences.

1. homework / she / doing / avoids / her

   ______________________________.

2. practicing / the / piano / continue / you / should

   ______________________________.

3. spelling / English / is / hard / words

   ______________________________.

4. they / cooking / hate / about / learning

   ______________________________.

5. classmates / likes / David / working / his / with

   ______________________________.

6. prefer / at / I / food court / eating / the

   ______________________________.

F Use the Language

Likes and dislikes

Write a paragraph about things you like and don't like about school life. Include classroom activities, studying at home, social activities, clubs, and athletics. When you're finished, discuss your paragraph with a partner.

Check Your Progress

1 **Complete the crossword with the gerund forms of the verbs in the box.**

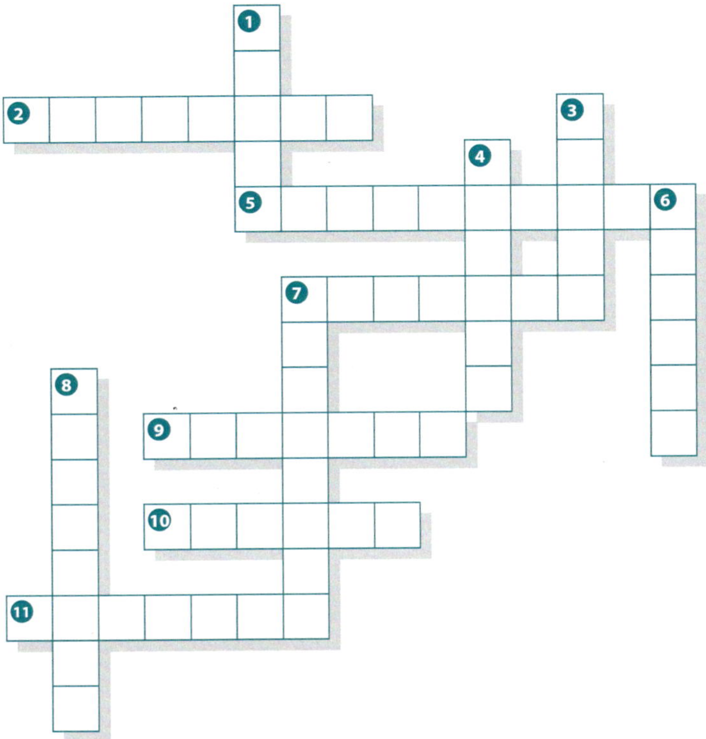

Across →

2. laugh
5. graduate
7. solve
9. read
10. make
11. sit

Down ↓

1. do
3. go
4. take
6. give
7. study
8. enjoy

2 **Read the email. Fill in the blanks with the correct words from the box.**

dislike	taking	love	solving	listening	discussing	doing

Hi, Kimberly!
I really like Southview University! I (1) ______________ studying science. My chemistry teachers are all very nice, and (2) ______________ experiments is a lot of fun. But I (3) ______________ studying mathematics. (4) ______________ math problems bores me. I also hate (5) ______________ to lectures and (6) ______________ notes. I prefer (7) ______________ things with my classmates.
Sorry. I'm complaining a lot. I really do like it here. I hope you're enjoying your new campus, too! Let's talk on the phone soon.
Best,
Tracey

3 **Read the email again and circle the correct answers.**

1. What does Tracey love? a. studying science b. studying mathematics
2. What does Tracey think is fun? a. doing experiments b. solving math problems
3. What does Tracey dislike? a. studying mathematics b. talking on the phone
4. What does Tracey prefer? a. taking notes b. discussing things

2E What Are You Up To?

A Model Conversation

Read the conversation. Then listen. Track 021

Nancy: Are you enjoying your semester?
Will: Yeah. I'm learning a lot and making friends. My roommate and I get along, too.
Nancy: Are you doing any extracurricular activities these days?
Will: Sure. I'm on a bowling team. We practice a lot on the weekends, so I'm improving my game. What about you?
Nancy: I'm in an English conversation club. We talk a lot about current events, news stories, movies—things like that.
Will: Are you doing it as part of a class?
Nancy: No. I'm taking English classes too, but the club is just for fun. We don't study—it's just chatting. My listening and speaking skills are really improving.
Will: That sounds great. Can I join?

B Vocabulary

Write the words and phrases next to the correct definitions.

improve	roommate	currently	club	skill	join
extracurricular activity	current event	at the moment	get along	chat	these days

1. something you choose to do at school but not for a class ____________
2. the ability to do something ____________
3. something happening recently or not long ago ____________
4. a social group for people with the same interest ____________
5. a person you live with ____________
6. to get better or make (something) better ____________
7. to become a member of (a club, team, etc.) ____________
8. to like each other; to enjoy being with each other ____________
9. to make conversation ____________
10. three phrases meaning *at this time* ____________ ____________ ____________

C In Your World

Answer the questions in one or two sentences.

1. Are you currently learning anything new? ____________

____

2. Who do you not get along with? ____________

____

D Grammar

Present continuous and related time expressions

statements: S + *be* + verb-*ing*...	
They **are talking** to their professor right now.	**I'm** not **studying** mathematics this semester.
yes/no questions: *Be* + S + verb-*ing*...?	
Are you **going** to class this morning?	**Is** she **doing** any extracurricular activities?
when and how to use present continuous	
• Use the present continuous to talk about what is happening right now. • Use it to talk about something that is current and temporary. For example: *I'm learning to play the violin—not at this moment, but these days. I'm living in the dormitory this semester.* Both of these sentences bring attention to something current. • Present continuous sentences often use expressions about a recent or current time.	
common time expressions	
now, at the moment, right now, today, tonight, nowadays, this ____ (minute, morning, week, semester, year)	

E Grammar Practice

Fill in the blanks to make questions. Match the questions and answers. Then fill in the blanks to complete the answers.

1. ________ he reading a book? •
2. ________ they studying Arabic this semester? •
3. ________ my singing improving? •
4. ________ I asking too many questions? •

• **a.** No, ________ not.
• **b.** Yes, ________ getting much better!
• **c.** Yes, ________ ________ a history book.
• **d.** No, ________ not ________ any language.

F Write to Speak

Now look back at the conversation in part A and circle all the words that end in *-ing*. Which are gerunds, and which are verbs? List three examples of each in the box below.

gerunds (used as nouns)	*-ing* verbs (used with *be*)

G Use the Language

These days

- Write a short list of things you're doing these days. What are you studying? How are you spending your free time? Keep your list a secret—don't show it to anyone!
- Find a partner. Give hints to help your partner guess some things on your list.
- Try to guess what your partner is doing these days. Then ask for some details.

Check Your Progress

1 Fill in the blanks with the correct words from the box.

doing	getting	chatting	taking	improving	learning

1. Please be quiet. We're ______________________ a history test at the moment.
2. I'm ______________________ my math skills by solving extra problems.
3. Are you ______________________ anything tonight? I need help with my homework.
4. He's ______________________ to play the piano. He can already play the violin.
5. Are you ______________________ along with your new roommate?
6. She's ______________________ online with a friend about college life.

2 Match the questions and answers.

1. What are they doing now? •
2. Are you going to the library today? •
3. Are you living in the dormitory? •
4. What are Steven and Jon doing tonight? •
5. Is he saying much in class these days? •

- • **a.** No, I'm not. I'm going there tomorrow.
- • **b.** They're playing soccer tonight.
- • **c.** Yes, he is. He talks a lot and asks questions this semester.
- • **d.** They're studying English at the moment.
- • **e.** Yes, I am. My building is beside the housing office.

3 Answer the questions with information that is true for you. Then discuss your answers with a partner.

1. What are you currently studying? ______________________
2. What are you doing tonight? ______________________
3. What are you doing this week? ______________________
4. Are you learning to play an instrument? ______________________
5. Are you living in the dormitory this year? ______________________

4 Read the student profiles. Circle the correct words. Then listen and check. Track 022

I'm Jane, and I'm (study / studying) mathematics. I'm also taking Russian classes. I enjoy doing many extracurricular activities. I (like / dislike) design, so I want to join a design club.

I'm Tamara. I'm studying music. I'm learning to play the guitar and the violin (this morning / this semester). I want to join the school band, so I'm practicing a lot (these days / this minute).

My name is Mike. I'm studying physics and chemistry. I (love / hate) science. I want to join the science club. I'm also thinking of (join / joining) an engineering club.

2F Courses and Electives

A Model Conversation

Read the conversation. Then listen. Track 023

Stacy: Why are you taking an economics class this semester? Aren't you a history major?
Brad: I am. Studying economics helps me understand a lot of historical events. Money is important, you know.
Stacy: Haha. I do know. What other classes are you taking?
Brad: For my major, I'm taking a class called South America in the 1800s.
Stacy: Huh. That sounds like a good elective for me. Who's the teacher?
Brad: Professor Williams. This week we're doing group presentations about industry and agriculture.
Stacy: How are you doing in that class?
Brad: I'm doing all right. I like the topic, but Professor Williams gives us a lot of extra reading assignments. Sometimes it's hard to keep up.

B Vocabulary

Write the words next to the correct definitions.

keep up	topic	industry	agriculture
historical	presentation	elective	assignment

1. work that a teacher or boss tells you to do ______________
2. the making or building of things in a factory ______________
3. related to history ______________
4. what a class, lecture, book, etc. is about; a subject ______________
5. a course not related to your major that you can choose to study ______________
6. to move or work at the same speed as others; to go fast enough ______________
7. farming; the raising of crops ______________
8. a short talk about a topic, sometimes by a student or group of students ______________

C In Your World

Think about one of your academic goals—for example, to learn another language or to improve your grades in a subject. Fill in the table below. Then discuss your goal with a partner.

My Goal: ______________________	
Good things about this goal: ______________ ______________ ______________	Difficult things about this goal: ______________ ______________ ______________

D Grammar

Present continuous in information questions

information questions: *Wh-* word + *be* + S + verb-*ing*...?		
questions	**short answers**	**long answers**
Where are we **going**? **What** classes **is** she **taking**? **How are** you **doing** in that class? **Why are** you **leaving**?	To the food court. History and economics. All right. Because I have class now.	We're going **to the food court**. She's taking **history and economics**. I'm doing **all right**. I'm leaving **because I have class now**.
subject questions: *Who* + *be* + verb-*ing*...?		
Who's teaching that class?	Professor Williams (is).	**Professor Williams** is teaching it.

Brief note

Present continuous questions can often be answered with just the subject, the matching form of *be*, and, if necessary, the word *not*.

E Grammar Practice

Write the beginning of each question below, including the correct form of *be*. One question is a yes/no question. Others use a word from the box below.

who	what	when	where	how	why

1. Q: __________ __________ you taking that class? A: Every weekday morning.
2. Q: __________ __________ he improving his English? A: He's taking a conversation class.
3. Q: __________ they sleeping? A: Yes, they are.
4. Q: __________ __________ you reading? A: I'm reading a science book.
5. Q: __________ __________ you carrying a guitar? A: Because I'm in a music club.
6. Q: __________ __________ Tom and Sarah going? A: To the financial aid center.
7. Q: __________ __________ talking on the phone? A: My roommate is.

F Read to Speak

Prepare to discuss some current events with your classmates. Research a few news stories about things that are happening in the world, and think of events at your school or in your city, too. Copy the headlines of some news stories about these events below.

____

____

____

G Use the Language

What's going on?

Now talk with other students in groups of two to five. Talk about what is happening in your school, your community, and your country. Ask and answer follow-up questions to get more details. You can follow this with a further discussion of what is going on internationally.

Check Your Progress

1 Listen to the conversation and fill in the blanks. Track 024

1. What's the ________________ for our world geography class?
2. Yeah, but I'm taking geography as an ________________ this semester.
3. I'm joining the class two weeks late, so it's hard to ________________ ________________.
4. And remember, we're giving our ________________ next week.
5. It's ________________ in North America. What's your ________________?

2 Listen again and choose the correct answers.

1.	What is Ezra majoring in?	a. geography	b. fine arts
2.	What is the assignment for tomorrow?	a. a presentation	b. reading
3.	Where are Ezra and Caroline going to meet?	a. the library	b. the bookstore
4.	What are they going to do there?	a. research	b. read

3 Fill in the blanks with *who*, *what*, *when*, *where*, *how*, or *why*.

	Q	A
1.	Q: ________ is she going to the food court?	A: She has a part-time job there.
2.	Q: ________ are we playing soccer at the athletic center?	A: After lunch.
3.	Q: ________ is she waiting to talk to?	A: Her physics professor.
4.	Q: ________ are you doing in the library?	A: Studying for a test.
5.	Q: ________ many classes are you taking this semester?	A: Six.
6.	Q: ________ are you living this year?	A: In an apartment off campus.

4 Read the answers. Then write questions about the underlined information.

1. What ________________________________? A: I am studying <u>English and music</u>.
2. ________________________________? A: He is going <u>to the housing office</u>.
3. ________________________________? A: I'm emailing her <u>to ask a question</u>.
4. ________________________________? A: <u>Dr. Patel</u> is giving the lecture.

2G Extracurricular Activities

A Authentic Text: A club poster

Read the poster. Then listen. Track 025

THE WYOMING STATE UNIVERSITY HORSE RIDING CLUB is looking for new members—and we want **YOU!**

We love horses. Do you? Then join us! We always have something exciting happening—every day of the week. Senior members of our club teach horse care, riding, and sports involving horses. We often have group rides, and you can always find a riding partner. This semester, our university is building a larger riding area, and it is opening in April. Do you want to take part in something really special? We usually have two riding events per semester, and more than twenty horses and riders participate. We hope to see you and your beautiful horse at a Horse Riding Club meeting soon!

Brief note

"Take part in" and *participate in* have the same meaning.

For more information, call 555-722-6262 or email at joinclub@wyomingacademic.com.

B Vocabulary

Fill in the blanks with the correct words from the box. Circle the correct adverbs of frequency.

special	take part	involving	event	participate	per	
Adverbs of Frequency						
never	hardly ever	occasionally	sometimes	often	usually	always

1. Today is a(n) ______________ day—we're watching a movie in class. We (often / hardly ever) watch movies!
2. I don't have time to ______________ in club activities. I (occasionally / always) study after classes and on weekends.
3. There's a social ______________ at the dorm every Friday night. It's (usually / never) a lot of fun!
4. Samantha loves doing experiments ______________ chemistry. She's (hardly ever / often) at the laboratory.
5. The classes at my college are (never / sometimes) very big. There are only about twenty students ______________ class, and the biggest classes have around thirty.

C In Your World

Talk with a partner about the extracurricular activities below. What do you think the members do? Which one would you like to join, and which would you not like to join? Explain your choices.

Skiing Team	School Newspaper	Hip-Hop Club
Yoga Club	Creative Writing Club	Future Business Leaders

D Quick Review

Look back at the brief notes in this module.

1. Which word has a different meaning than the others? (job occupation lecture career)
2. To ask about someone's (occupation / department), say (*What do you do?* / *What are you doing?*)

E Grammar

> **Brief note**
> A *routine* is the things you usually do and the order you do them in.

Simple present vs. present continuous

simple present	present continuous
Use for routines: *I **take** the bus to school every day.* Use for facts that are generally true at all times: *Students **study**.*	Use for something happening now: *Harry **is talking** with his sociology professor.* Use for something current and temporary: *I'**m learning** a lot this semester.*

stative verbs

- Many verbs do not describe an action. Examples include *be* and *hate*. These verbs are called stative verbs. We usually use stative verbs in the simple present tense, NOT in the present continuous.
- Stative verbs include most verbs that discuss what you know, think, or feel (*I **like** this soup.*), what you believe (*I don't **believe** you.*), what you see or hear (*I **see** a snake!*), what you own (*I **have** a car.*), or just ways of being. They don't discuss actions.

> **Brief note**
> A good way to learn which verbs do not use present continuous is by listening to how native English speakers use them.

> **Brief note**
> Some stative verbs can be used in the present continuous tense when they imply an action.
> *I'm having lunch with my friend.*
> *I'm thinking of my mom now.*

F Grammar Practice

Fill in the blanks with the correct forms of the verbs.

1. (like) Carlos ______________ playing soccer.
2. (watch) At the moment, I ______________ a video lecture.
3. (study) They ______________ for next week's test.
4. (sit) That's her. She ______________ near the back of the class.
5. (know) ______________ you ______________ a lot about geography?
6. (fit) This jacket ______________ not ______________ me well.
7. (believe) We ______________ exercising every day is good for you.
8. (have) He ______________ many cousins.
9. (rain) Look out the window. ______________ it ______________?
10. (work) I ______________, so I can't meet you for lunch today.

G Use the Language

How often?

Ask a partner these questions and mark his or her responses in the table. Follow up by asking a few questions of your own.

Questionnaire: How often do you do the following? (Put a check mark in the correct box.)	Always	Often	Sometimes	Never
1. go home right after school	☐	☐	☐	☐
2. copy class notes from a classmate	☐	☐	☐	☐
3. study outside with classmates	☐	☐	☐	☐
4. eat lunch in a school cafeteria	☐	☐	☐	☐
5. participate in class discussions	☐	☐	☐	☐
6. attend a club/team meeting	☐	☐	☐	☐

When both you and your partner have completed your questionnaires, survey your other classmates and compare the results. Survey the entire class. What answers did most students give? Is there anything that everyone always does? Is there something that nobody ever does?

Check Your Progress

1 **Fill in the blanks with the correct words from the box.**

taking part	hardly ever	per	involving	sometimes	special	event	usually

1. The next big club ________________ is on April 3rd.
2. Are you doing anything ________________ on your birthday?
3. My phys. ed. class is easy. We ________________ ________________ have homework.
4. I like spending time in the lab, so I look for classes ________________ experiments.
5. With this meal plan, you get two meals ________________ day.
6. Edward loves ________________ ________________ in class discussions.
7. She can't see well, so she ________________ sits at the front of the class.
8. Don't study all the time! Take a break ________________.

2 **Underline the errors and rewrite the sentences correctly.**

1. I'm liking participating in Business Club events.

   ____

2. Do you learn a lot this semester?

   ____

3. The yoga club doesn't meet at the moment.

   ____

4. This dormitory is having six floors.

   ____

5. The drama club is occasionally practicing on the quad.

   ____

3 **Read the email. Then write an email to a friend about parts of your routine. Use adverbs of frequency.**

Hi, Mary.

I'm very busy at school these days. I'm a member of the Hip-Hop Club, the school newspaper, and the Creative Writing Club. The Hip-Hop Club usually meets three days per week. We often meet in the student center, play music, and dance. The school newspaper always meets in the library on Mondays and Wednesdays. I attend Creative Writing Club meetings one day per week. It's my favorite club, so I never miss a meeting.

Beth

Hi ____________

____

____

____

____

____

____

____

____

Unit Review

A An Educational Questionnaire

Read the completed questionnaire. Then put a check mark (✓) next to true or false.

1. What is your name? Gary Jackson
2. Are you currently a student? (Y/N) No
   If yes, then what is your current grade or year in university? ______ Class of ______
   What are you studying? ______
   Which school are you attending? ______
   If no, then what is the name of the last school you attended? New York University
   Did you graduate? Yes Class of 2024
   What was your major? Film Studies
3. What is the highest level of education you completed?
   Graduated university with a bachelor's degree

1. Gary is currently attending university.	☐ true	☐ false
2. Gary finished graduate school in 2024.	☐ true	☐ false
3. Gary studied movies.	☐ true	☐ false

Write more questions about what someone is currently doing at school, studying, etc., to add to the survey. Leave the answers blank for now.

4. ______________________________?
   ______________________________.
5. ______________________________?
   ______________________________.
6. ______________________________?
   ______________________________.

B An Oral Survey

Interview a partner to get his or her answers to your survey questions above. Ask and answer using complete sentences. Then write short, simple answers based on your partner's responses.

C Reminder

Put a check mark (✓) next to the things you can do.

______ Find basic information in posters or advertisements
______ Describe what you like doing and don't like (for example, with regard to school)
______ Complete a questionnaire with information about your educational background

Further Practice

A Listen to Write

For a class assignment, Wendy is writing a paragraph about what she is doing these days. Read, listen, and fill in the blanks. Track 026

I ______________ high school last spring, and now I'm a freshman at Penn State. I ______________ ______________ in world history. ______________ ______________ in a dormitory ______________ the Weaver Building. Many of my history classes are in that building. I ______________ walk along the path between the library and the theater to get to class. But ______________ ______________ ______________ off campus to visit a café before classes. ______________, I don't have much time to spend in the café. That's because ______________ ______________ for a big midterm test this week, so I'm spending a lot of time in the library between classes. And I ______________ stay in my dorm room in the evenings to study. Last semester, I was in the Spanish ______________ and on the basketball team. But now I'm very busy, so I'm not ______________ in extracurricular activities much ______________ ______________. I ______________ need a break from studying, so I meet my friends to have coffee or lunch and to ______________.

B Prewrite

Use the space below to list five or six of your recent activities. Then select the three most interesting ones and think about how to describe them.

C Now Write

Write a short paragraph about your recent activities. Look back at part A for help if necessary.

MEMO

UNIT 3 Exploring New Places

Scan and find the tracks.

Before You Read

◆ **Talk about these questions with your classmates.**

1. How do you greet someone when meeting for the first time?
2. How do you greet a friend?
3. How do you feel when someone stands too close when they talk to you?

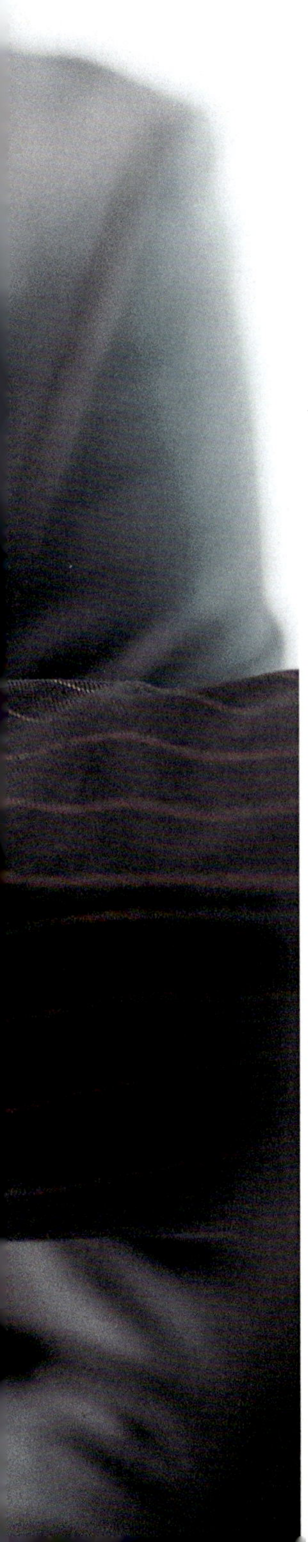

Vocabulary

◆ **Read the definitions. Then match each word in bold with its definition.**

A. to touch with an open hand in a gentle, friendly way
B. a real or imaginary point beyond which a person can't go or do something
C. causing embarrassment or tension
D. the gesture of bending the head or body forward
E. something friendly or nice that you say or do when you meet someone
F. a round, ball-like area usually filled with air
G. to wrap your arms around someone and hold them tightly
H. not able to be seen
I. on or associated with the face
J. the sound people make when they are happy or something is funny

1. _____ Some friends **hug** as a greeting.
2. _____ **Greetings** can say a lot about personal space across cultures.
3. _____ People have an **invisible** space around themselves that they consider their own.
4. _____ Some friends **pat** each other on the back when greeting.
5. _____ If you invade someone's space, they may respond with stiff **laughter**.
6. _____ Some people **bow**, but others kiss when they greet each other.
7. _____ Invasion of space may result in **awkward** silence.
8. _____ Respect for their **boundaries** makes people feel comfortable.
9. _____ Every person is surrounded by a **bubble** of their own space.
10. _____ If you get too close to someone, they may make a strange **facial** expression.

Culture and Personal Space

Track 027

People tend to stand a certain distance apart while talking. We all have an invisible bubble of space around ourselves that we consider to be our own. Usually, we feel uncomfortable when someone enters our personal space. How much space individuals need differs by culture. This can lead to some interesting intercultural communication.

There are basically two different kinds of cultures in the world: contact and non-contact. Contact cultures are groups that tend to stand close together and touch often. The Middle East and South America are home to many examples of contact cultures. Non-contact cultures are groups that tend to want more space and do not touch very often. The Far East, Great Britain, and the United States are examples of non-contact cultures.

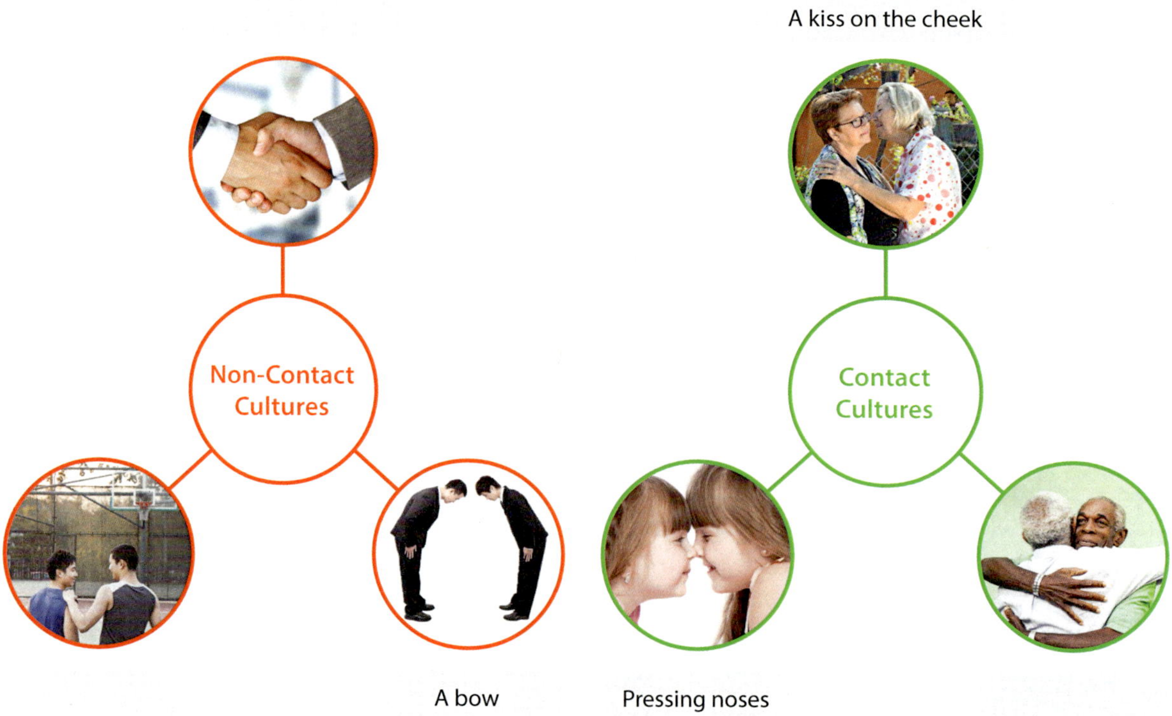

▲ Greetings in contact and non-contact cultures

Learning to be aware of cultural understandings about space helps us interact successfully. Greetings tell a lot about personal space in different cultures. People in many cultures use a handshake when meeting someone for the first time. Others bow, and still others give kisses on either one or both cheeks. A person who usually bows in greeting might be surprised to receive a kiss on the cheek from a stranger. Greetings among friends can also be different. Some friends hug, some pat each other on the back, and yet others press their noses together.

It is important to recognize and understand social cues given off by people from other cultures. If you notice someone moving away from you while talking, give them space. Their personal bubble is bigger than yours! Other cues include stiff laughter, strange facial expressions, and awkward silences. Respecting boundaries is a way to make people feel comfortable. And it is helpful in making friends with people from all over the world.

Review the Highlights

◆ **Mark up the text and infographic according to the instructions.**

1. Look at Paragraph 1. Circle what determines how much space individuals need.
2. Look at Paragraph 2. Put stars next to the names of places that are home to many contact cultures.
3. Look at Paragraph 3. Circle all of the different kinds of greetings mentioned.
4. Look at Paragraph 4. Underline the social cues people might give off when feeling uncomfortable.
5. Look at Paragraph 4. Underline the reasons why it is important to be aware of personal space.
6. Look at the infographic. Use the information in the reading to label the pictures in the infographic.

Check Your Comprehension

◆ **Circle the correct answer.**

1. How are personal space and culture related? Details: how
   a. Each country has its own laws about these things.
   b. The amount of space people need varies by culture.
   c. There is a link between personal space and language.
   d. They are not related.

2. Which is NOT an example of a non-contact culture? Negative fact
   a. The United States
   b. Great Britain
   c. The Far East
   d. The Middle East

3. According to the infographic, what are two examples of greetings in contact cultures? Fact
   a. Two kisses on the cheek / A handshake
   b. A pat on the back / A bow
   c. A kiss on the cheek / A hug
   d. A handshake / Pressing noses together

4. How could someone show you that you are too close to him or her? Details: how
   a. With a smile and a normal facial expression
   b. By walking closer to you
   c. With a pat on the shoulder
   d. By laughing uncomfortably

5. Why is it important to respect the boundaries of others? Details: why
   a. It helps you make friends and be liked by different kinds of people.
   b. It keeps you from interacting successfully with different kinds of people.
   c. It makes people feel uncomfortable.
   d. It shows people that you have visited their country before.

◆ **Complete the summary. Write the words from the reading that best fit in the blanks. One word is extra.**

patting bubble boundaries facial bowing invisible awkwardly greetings

Every person has a 1. ______________ of personal space. When this space is invaded, someone might move away, make strange 2. ______________ expressions, or become 3. ______________ silent. How much space people need depends on their culture. Contact cultures, such as those in the Middle East and South America, tend to stand close together and touch often. However, people from non-contact cultures tend to need more space and touch less. Learning to be aware of differences helps us interact with each other successfully. 4. ______________ are one way that we interact. Different cultures greet by shaking hands, 5. ______________, hugging, or 6. ______________ each other on the back. By respecting the personal 7. ______________ of others, we make people feel comfortable and make friends easily.

Linked Skills Activity

◆ **Listen to the conversation and complete the summary.** Track 028

Julie went to 1. ______________ for the summer, and she noticed a lot of cultural 2. ______________. Many things were different than what she was used to. She found it interesting that food delivered to houses doesn't come on 3. ______________ plates or in containers. It is delivered on regular 4. ______________, and then the plates are picked up later. She also enjoyed the group culture. She never felt alone and she always felt 5. ______________. It was nice to experience a culture where people do most things as a group. Everyone was always doing fun things together, so it was easy to make 6. ______________.

◆ **With a partner, talk about cultural differences that you have experienced. Write examples for each category.**

Interesting Differences	Negative Differences	Unusual Differences

◆ **Choose a culture that you are familiar with and prepare a speech to your classmates about some of the cultural differences between that culture and your own. Include a variety of cultural differences.**

Speech Notes

The International Lounge: A Global Hub on Campus

Track 029

[KMU Core Competency: Cultural Awareness]

Established in 2005, the International Lounge at Keimyung University is a vibrant space where local and international students can come together to share ideas, exchange traditions, and learn from each other. It offers a unique environment for students to connect with people from around the world, whether they are looking to practice languages, explore different cultures, or build lifelong friendships.

Managed by both Korean and international students, the lounge provides a global atmosphere that fosters mutual respect and understanding. Programs such as the Korean Language and Culture Exchange (KLACE) and International Day give students opportunities to experience new perspectives and engage with diverse cultures. Regular events like conversation clubs and cultural workshops further encourage meaningful interactions and help students feel part of a supportive community.

The lounge also features inviting spaces to help students feel comfortable and welcome. With cozy seating, a café zone, and an outdoor deck, it is the perfect place to relax, collaborate, or simply spend time with others. These amenities create an environment that supports personal growth, strengthens community bonds, and makes cultural exchange a natural part of campus life.

Since its establishment, the International Lounge has represented Keimyung University's commitment to inclusivity and **cultural awareness**. It is a space where diversity thrives, and students can broaden their horizons while contributing to a dynamic international community.

Check Your Comprehension

1. What is the purpose of the International Lounge?
   (A) To encourage international and Korean students to learn languages
   (B) To encourage students to share and learn about their home cultures
   (C) To encourage participation in university and community events
   (D) All of the above

2. Which service is NOT offered by the International Lounge?
   (A) Learning Advisory Support classes
   (B) Foreign exchange travel
   (C) Information on international cultures
   (D) Korean Language and Culture Exchange

3. Which program at the International Lounge focuses specifically on learning about Korean culture?
   (A) Conversation Clubs
   (B) International Day
   (C) Korean Language and Culture Exchange (KLACE)
   (D) Cultural Workshops

Talk or Write about It

1. Describe a place you have traveled to. What made it special?

   ____

   ____

2. If you could visit any country, which one would you choose?

   ____

   ____

3. What are some challenges exchange students might face when living in a new country?

   ____

   ____

3C Thinking about a Trip

A Model Conversation

Read the conversation. Then listen. Track 030

Cathy: Wow, look at this picture. My friend is traveling in Asia right now. I want to go on a trip.

Max: Me too. That looks amazing. Where do you want to go?

Cathy: Hmm. I want to go somewhere off the beaten path.

Max: I do too. Let's check online for some exciting tours.

Cathy: Great idea. Oh, take a look at this. How about riding a camel in the desert in Morocco?

Max: Uh, I don't know... What about exploring the jungles of Costa Rica?

Cathy: That sounds cool, too. There are a lot of options for thrill-seekers like us.

Brief note

"Me too" and "I do too" show that you agree with someone.

B Vocabulary

Match the expressions to the correct definitions.

1. thrill-seeker •
2. explore •
3. off the beaten path •
4. option •
5. tour •

- • **a.** a trip through a new place
- • **b.** one of two or more choices
- • **c.** a person who likes to do exciting things
- • **d.** to travel around a place to learn about it
- • **e.** in a place where not many people go

C Vocabulary Comprehension

Fill in the blanks with the correct words and phrases from the box.

desert	tours	camel	explore	options	jungle	off the beaten path

1. Cathy wants to go ____________________ on her trip.
2. Max wants to see the ____________________ in Costa Rica.
3. Cathy wants to ride a(n) ____________________ in the desert.
4. Max is looking on the Internet for ____________________.
5. There is a ____________________ in Morocco.
6. There are a lot of ____________________ available to Max and Cathy.
7. Max and Cathy are thrill-seekers. They like to ____________________ new places.

D Grammar

Making suggestions with *let's* + verb or *What about / How about* + verb + *-ing*

making suggestions using *let's*	making suggestions with *What about / How about* + verb + *-ing*
Use *let's* + the base form of the verb.	**Use *what* or *how* + *about* + the *-ing* form of the verb.**
Let's check online for tours. **Let's ride** a camel in the desert.	**What about exploring** the jungles of Costa Rica? **How about going** on a tour?

Brief note

Let's is short for *Let us*, but don't say *Let us*. It's hardly ever used.

E Grammar Practice

Circle the correct answers.

1. How about (going / go) to New York in December?
2. What about (take / taking) a tour of the new university campus?
3. Let's (travel / traveling) to the jungles of Brazil.
4. What about (visiting / visit) my aunt and uncle in Egypt?
5. (Let's / Let) book a trip to Costa Rica for next summer.
6. How about (going / go) to China to see the Great Wall?

F Use the Language

Suggesting where to travel

With a partner, suggest three places to travel to:

1. ______________________________
2. ______________________________
3. ______________________________

Now suggest some things that a person can do in each place, together or alone. Discuss your ideas first, and then write down some interesting points from your conversation.

Place #1	Place #2	Place #3
______________	______________	______________
______________	______________	______________
______________	______________	______________
______________	______________	______________

Work with another group. With your partner, ask what the people in the other group like to do. Then suggest that they go to one of the places you discussed above. Where should they go? Do they want to go there?

Check Your Progress

1 **Match the words with their definitions.**

1. Morocco	•	• **a.** not visited by many people
2. off the beaten path	•	• **b.** a trip to explore a new place
3. jungle	•	• **c.** a person who likes doing exciting things
4. camel	•	• **d.** a country in the north part of Africa
5. tour	•	• **e.** a very dry area with few trees and little water
6. desert	•	• **f.** a very thick tropical forest, such as the ones in Costa Rica
7. thrill-seeker	•	• **g.** an animal with a round back; it usually lives in or near deserts

2 **Listen to the conversations. Then match them to the pictures. Write *a*, *b*, *c*, or *d* in the blanks.** Track 031

______

______

______

______

3 **Underline the errors and write the correct word(s) on the lines.**

1. How about we staying in this hotel?

______

2. Let's to check online for options.

______

3. Let's finding a cheap tour of the Amazon.

______

4. How about take a train?

______

4 **Put the conversation in the correct order. Then listen and check.** Track 032

__1__ **Maria:** So, what did you find online?

____ **Maria:** That sounds amazing. Let's go there.

____ **Ricardo:** Sounds good!

____ **Maria:** Oh, what is it?

____ **Maria:** You're right. Hey, what about going to Argentina this year and exploring Costa Rica next year?

____ **Maria:** That sounds cool, too! How about doing both?

____ **Ricardo:** Well, there's a tour of Patagonia in Argentina. It's really beautiful. It's in a lot of movies.

____ **Ricardo:** Exploring the jungle in Costa Rica.

____ **Ricardo:** You know that's too expensive.

____ **Ricardo:** Wait. There's another option.

3D Deciding on a Trip

A Model Conversation

Read the conversation. Then listen. Track 033

Max: Okay, Cathy, where are we going to go? There are so many cool places to visit.

Cathy: Here, this ad for India looks interesting.

Max: Hmm, I don't want to go to India in the summer. It's too hot.

Cathy: Oh, good point. Me neither. I hate extreme heat.

Max: China seems exciting. My sister is traveling there next year.

Cathy: Really? Are your parents visiting her when she's there?

Max: I'm not sure. They don't like Chinese food very much.

Cathy: I don't either. It's too spicy for me.

Max: I'm having Chinese for dinner tonight—yum!

Brief note

"Good point" means, "That's true; you're right."

B Vocabulary

Match the words with the correct definition.

1. ad
2. extreme
3. spicy
4. hate

- **a.** having a strong, hot flavor, often from peppers
- **b.** a promotion for a product or service
- **c.** to feel strong dislike or anger toward someone or something
- **d.** very intense or beyond the usual limits

C In Your World

Think about your country's weather and food. Write down what you like and what you hate. Then talk with a partner. Write down your partner's answers.

For example:

A: I hate the cold weather in the winter. How about you?

B: I love the cold, but I don't like the extreme heat in the summer.

Weather I like: ____________________

____

Weather I hate: ____________________

____

Food I love: ____________________

____

Food I don't like: ____________________

____

Weather my partner likes: ____________________

____

Weather my partner hates: ____________________

____

Food my partner loves: ____________________

____

Food my partner doesn't like: ____________________

____

D Grammar

Discussing the future; showing agreement

present continuous with future meaning
S + *be* + verb-*ing*
I am having Chinese food for dinner **tonight**. **My sister is traveling** to China **next year**.

agreement	
with positive statements	**with negative statements**
A: I love Japanese food. B: **Me too. / I do too!**	A: I don't like spicy food. B: **Me neither. / I don't either.**

E Grammar Practice

Put the words in order to make sentences.

1. Italian / I / am / dinner / for / having / tomorrow / night

   ______________________________.

2. we / meeting / our / are / tonight / parents

   ______________________________.

3. going / my / trip / is / on / month / next / a / friend

   ______________________________.

4. I / this / to / am / interview / tomorrow / wearing / the

   ______________________________.

Complete the conversations with the correct agreement phrases. Then practice with a partner.

5. **Mary:** I really love hot weather! **Joe:** ______________
6. **Duncan:** I don't enjoy the winters—they get so cold! **Sophia:** ______________

F Use the Language

And you?

Write sentences about things you like or don't like and what you're going to do in the future. Then find three people and discuss your sentences. Write a check mark when people agree with you and an *X* when they disagree. Keep the discussion going with follow-up questions. Share your answers with the class.

Statement	Names		
	______	______	______
I hate…			
I really like…			
I…			
I…			
I…			

Check Your Progress

1 Fill in the blanks with the words from the box.

China	extreme heat	spicy	hate	extreme cold	yum

1. This food is too ______________. I don't think I can eat it.
2. My parents are from ______________, so I'd like to go there.
3. Samantha hates the ______________ ______________ here in Canada. She always goes to Miami in winter.
4. ______________! This chocolate cake is so good.
5. The weather here is terrible. I ______________ it.
6. I don't like ______________ ______________ either, but it's okay when I'm on the beach in India!

2 Choose the correct answers.

1. I don't like doing exciting things. I'm not a thrill-seeker. a. Me too. b. Me neither.
2. I like Chinese food, but I love Indian food. a. I do too. b. I don't either.
3. I think extreme heat is better than extreme cold. a. I do too. b. Me neither.
4. It's raining, and I don't have an umbrella. a. Me too. b. I don't either.
5. I want to go to China in the spring. a. Me too. b. Me neither.

3 Listen to the conversation. What are the women NOT planning to do? Choose the correct answer. Track 034

a. stay in California

b. see the desert

c. visit Las Vegas

4 Listen again. Are these statements true (t) or false (f)?

1. The woman and her sister are flying to LA. ______
2. They are leaving on Saturday. ______
3. They're flying from LA to Las Vegas. ______
4. The sisters want to see the desert in Arizona. ______
5. The man wants to go to the Grand Canyon. ______
6. They are driving from Montana to LA. ______
7. The man wants the woman to send him pictures. ______

5 Write the correct forms of the verbs. Then circle the words or phrases that show the speaker is discussing the future.

1. We ______________ ______________ (go) to France next year.
2. I ______________ ______________ (take) a tour of London in August.
3. ______________ ______________ ______________ (you, travel) to India this summer?
4. Jack ______________ ______________ (explore) the city this weekend.
5. My sister ______________ ______________ (leave) to go on a trip tomorrow.
6. ______________ ______________ ______________ (they, have) something spicy for dinner tonight?

3E What Could We Do on Vacation?

A Model Conversation

Read the conversation. Then listen. Track 035

Cathy: Here, Max. Look at this travel ad for Peru. It's really interesting. There are so many incredible things we could do.

Max: Yeah, that looks fantastic. We could hike along the Inca Trail.

Cathy: Or we could take a train and then hike into the jungle for a real adventure!

Max: We have to visit Machu Picchu. I could spend hours there. I'm a history fan.

Cathy: I couldn't stay that long. But you're right—we have to go. We could go there and then do the jungle hike.

Max: It says here we can take a riverboat along the Amazon, too.

Cathy: I can't go. I get sick on boats.

B Vocabulary Practice

Read the sentences. Match the underlined words to the correct definitions. One definition is used twice.

1. ______ I'm a history <u>fan</u>.
2. ______ Look at all the <u>incredible</u> things we can do.
3. ______ Yeah, that looks <u>fantastic</u>.
4. ______ I saw an <u>ad</u> in a magazine.
5. ______ We really had an <u>adventure</u> in Peru!

a. short form of the word *advertisement*
b. great; amazing
c. someone who really likes something
d. an exciting time

Now write a new sentence using each word. Then read your sentences to a partner.

ad: ______________________________

fan: ______________________________

fantastic: ______________________________

incredible: ______________________________

adventure: ______________________________

C In Your World

Discuss these questions with a partner. Then share your answers with another pair.

What do you like to do when you travel?

What are you a fan of? Why?

D Grammar

can for ability; *can* and *could* for possibility

can for ability: *can* + verb	*can* and *could* for possibility: *can/could* + verb
Use *can* to talk about ability—things you're able to do.	Use *can* or *could* to talk about possibility in the present or the future. *Could* means the same as *can* in this context but is less direct.
I **can speak** three languages: English, Spanish, and German. She **can't swim** very well.	We **can/could hike** along the Inca Trail, or we **can/could take** the train. We **can/could go** to Machu Picchu.

E Grammar Practice

Fill in the blanks with the correct words from the box.

can	speak	can't	hike	could	eat

1. Can you ______________________ French, too?
2. I ______________________ meet you at the station. See you there.
3. I ______________________ swim well. Let's not go to the river.
4. When we visit China, we ______________________ see the Great Wall.
5. He can't ______________________ spicy food—it hurts his stomach.
6. We could ______________________ up to the top of the mountain. The views are incredible, I'm sure.

F Use the Language

Could we go together?

Look at these travel ads. Think about which place you want to visit and why.

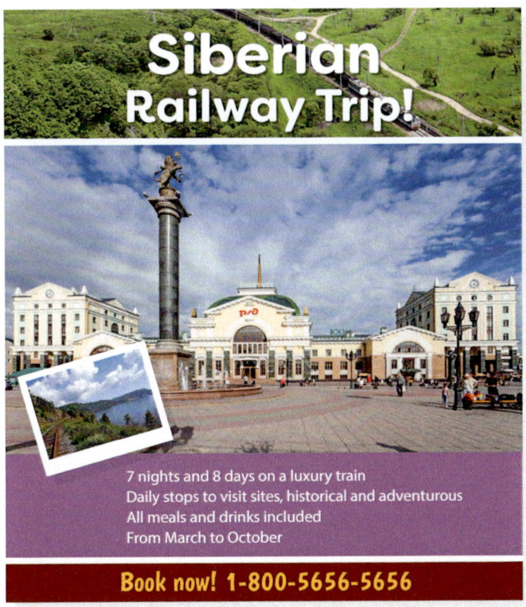

Now find a partner and ask where he or she wants to go. Talk about what you could do in each place. Do you have similar ideas? Do you want to travel together? Why or why not?

Check Your Progress

1 Choose the best pictures to match the statements.

1. That white jacket is fantastic. I could buy it for my trip. ______
2. You can see some incredible things in Nepal. ______
3. I'm a big fan of hiking and adventure. ______
4. We're visiting some friends. Their house is by a river. ______

2 Match the two columns to make sentences.

1. I could look	a. you at the subway station.
2. Can you	b. Portugal this winter.
3. Sheila can speak	c. at ads for adventure tours.
4. We could go to	d. Spanish very well.
5. My dad can't	e. go on the trip. He has to work.
6. I can meet	f could take the bus.
7. We don't have to walk. We	g. eat really spicy food?

3 Listen to each sentence and circle the word that you hear. Then check and practice.

Track 036

1. Jim (can / can't) swim.
2. We (can / can't) drive.
3. Ella (can / can't) travel now.
4. I (can / can't) speak Portuguese.
5. They (can / can't) pay for the trip.

4 Fill in the blanks with the correct words from the box.

incredible	hike	river	trails	fan	adventure	riverboat

Hi Derek,

How's it going? I'm planning a trip now. I checked a lot of ads and chose a trip to Vietnam. I remember that you went to Vietnam once. Could you please let me know what you think?

I found a lot of pictures of the jungles and old cities there. They look ❶ ______________! You know I'm a big ❷ ______________ of Asian history. On this trip, I could see a lot of old buildings in Hanoi, the capital city, and in other places. I can also ❸ ______________ outside the city. There are a lot of good ❹ ______________ for hikers. Then I could fly to Ho Chi Minh City, take a ❺ ______________ down the ❻ ______________ there, and go to Phu Quoc (Paradise Island). It sounds like a(n) ❼ ______________! What do you think?

Take care,
Sabina

3F Planning the Trip

A Authentic Text: An email exchange

Read the emails. Then listen. Track 037

To: Max <madmax@mail.com>
From: Cathy M <magiccathy@mail.com>
Date: Mon, Aug 15 at 9:21 PM
Subject: Trip

Hi, Max.

We need to call the travel agency ASAP to book our plane tickets. I can do that tomorrow morning. I don't have class, so I can call them and then let you know. We need to decide on specific dates for our trip. What do you think?

Cathy

To: Cathy M <magiccathy@mail.com>
From: Max <madmax@mail.com>
Date: Mon, Aug 15 at 10:07 PM
Subject: Re: Trip

Hi, Cathy.

Before you call the travel agency, I can do a quick search online tonight to compare prices. We need to find the best deal possible. After checking the prices, we can decide on the dates. Oh, and do we need to pay in person, or can we pay online?

Max

Brief note

"In person" means face to face—looking at the other person involved.

B Vocabulary

Listen to each word or phrase. Repeat. Then write the words and phrases next to the correct definitions. Track 038

travel agency book compare ASAP deal specific date quick ticket

Definition	Word(s)
the number of the day in the month (for example, October 1st)	
to look at two or more things in order to see how they are alike or different	
a place that sells vacations	
exact; particular	
to reserve; to schedule	
fast	
"as soon as possible" = quickly; right away	
a piece of paper that lets you travel on a bus, plane, train, etc.	
a good price	

C In Your World

Look online or in a newspaper. Find two travel ads. Use them to fill in the table.

Travel Ad #1	Travel Ad #2
Name of travel agency:	Name of travel agency:
Destination:	Destination:
Dates of travel:	Dates of travel:
Details:	Details:

Share your information with a partner.

D Grammar

can for offers and volunteering; *need to* for obligation

***can* for offers and volunteering** S + *can* + verb	***need to* for obligation** S + *need to* + verb
Use *can* to make offers or volunteer to do things.	Use *need to* like *have to*. Use it when you have an obligation (something you have to do).
I **can call** the travel agency tomorrow. I have some free time. I **can do** a quick search online to check prices.	We **need to call** the travel agency ASAP. It is necessary to get the tickets. Do we **need to pay** in person, or can we do it online?

Brief note

Here, *can* is used to make offers in statements.

E Grammar Practice

Underline the errors and write the correct word(s) on the lines.

1. I can calling you later with more information. ________________
2. She needs to remembering her passport. ________________
3. Do I need bring my book? ________________
4. He can doing a search on their website. ________________
5. We need to booked the tickets in advance. ________________
6. They needing to pack their suitcases. ________________
7. Mr. Brown can buying tickets online. ________________
8. My teacher can't not help us with the test. ________________
9. Can I helped you? ________________
10. Do we need to showing our passports? ________________

F Use the Language

Planning a trip

You and a partner want to plan a vacation. Choose a destination and make a list of things that you need to do to plan the trip.

To-Do List	
☐	☐
☐	☐
☐	☐
☐	☐

Share your travel plans and list with the class. Explain why you need to do those things.

Check Your Progress

1 Find and circle the words.

U	Q	X	A	E	T	A	D	R	T	Q	I	C	F	B
O	O	X	V	G	R	E	M	F	L	K	I	K	W	Q
N	H	W	X	B	E	R	S	O	U	F	V	S	N	J
W	L	R	T	G	W	N	I	R	I	G	Y	Y	D	Z
C	O	M	P	A	R	E	C	C	M	H	P	O	B	I
N	Z	I	I	V	I	R	E	Y	L	F	H	V	O	B
Y	J	G	B	M	B	P	D	K	Z	W	R	H	O	G
I	A	W	N	M	S	E	B	P	Q	I	E	N	K	J
X	I	P	J	B	A	M	Y	T	K	F	M	E	L	M
K	J	P	D	L	U	Q	T	E	A	X	T	S	N	K
C	Z	N	F	B	W	O	N	I	K	L	R	P	U	R
I	X	M	Z	A	V	O	F	G	C	K	H	Q	F	N
U	T	A	W	P	B	L	Y	Q	I	K	S	Z	O	E
Q	G	V	M	H	V	R	M	Z	W	N	E	C	F	O
H	R	W	Q	D	F	M	P	Y	Y	G	V	T	R	V

agency
book
quick
compare
date
deal
ticket
specific

2 Choose the sentence with the same meaning.

1. This Nepal tour is a real deal!
a. The tour price is too much.
b. The tour price is not expensive.

2. Let's compare prices.
a. We should see how the prices are different.
b. We should ask for a low price.

3. I can book the tickets online.
a. I can reserve the tickets on the Internet.
b. I can search for the tickets on the Internet.

4. What specific song do you want to hear?
a. I want to know the kind of song you want to hear.
b. I want to know the one song you want to hear.

3 Fill in the blanks with *need to* or *can*. Then listen and check. Track 039

1. We ____________ check the online deals soon. I ____________ do it after class.
2. There are no trains or airports there, so I ____________ rent a car. Then I ____________ drive you home.
3. I ____________ book the tickets. Do we ____________ come back before the end of the school break?
4. ____________ you compare prices on the website right now? I ____________ reserve the trip today.

4 Put the words in order to make sentences. Then write them again as negative sentences.

1. tickets / we / book / need / our / soon / to ____________________.
(*negative*) ____________________.
2. you / with / can / a / credit card / pay ____________________.
(*negative*) ____________________.
3. agency / can / call / I / travel / now / the ____________________.
(*negative*) ____________________.
4. he / the / on / to / decide / date / needs ____________________.
(*negative*) ____________________.

3G Let's Book Our Trip!

A Model Conversation

Read the conversation. Then listen. Track 040

Cathy: Okay, Max. Tell me where on the plane you want to sit.
Max: Please don't put me in a window seat. I'm afraid of heights.
Cathy: Really? Okay, it says, "Click here to reserve." Done.
Max: Don't close the window. It's still processing.
Cathy: Now it says, "Choose ticket type." Do we want to print our tickets, or do we want e-tickets?
Max: Don't print them. We can just bring our passports to the airport. They match the passport to the ticket number.
Cathy: Then don't forget to bring your passport.
Max: Of course. That's the most important thing.

B Vocabulary

Read each word or phrase, listen, and repeat. Then match each word or phrase to the correct picture. Track 041

afraid of heights (   )   click (   )   airport (   )   print (   )   passport (   )

C Vocabulary: On an airplane

Read. Then listen and practice. Track 042

Can you think of words for other parts of the airplane? Write them below. Then draw arrows to match them to the picture.

__________ __________ __________ __________ __________

D In Your World

Discuss these questions with a partner. Then share your answers with another pair.

Do you have experience traveling by airplane?
On an airplane, where do you like to sit?
Do/Would you like to fly? Why or why not?

E Grammar

Imperatives

Use imperatives to give commands, make suggestions, give instructions, or encourage someone.			
affirmative imperatives: verb (base form)		**negative imperatives:** ***Do not / Don't*** **+ verb**	
Take care.	(suggestion/farewell)	**Don't forget** your passport.	(command)
Be on time, please.	(command/instruction)	**Don't close** the window.	(instruction)
Tell me where you want to sit on the plane.	(command)	**Don't put** me in a window seat.	(command)
		Don't work too hard.	(suggestion/farewell)
Click here to save.	(instruction)	**Don't give up**.	(encouragement)

F Grammar Practice

Fill in the blanks with words from part E.

1. ______________ forget to pack a bathing suit. There's a beautiful pool at the hotel.
2. ______________ here to book your trip online.
3. Have a great trip. ______________ care!
4. ______________ faster. You need to finish this work quickly.
5. Don't ______________ the window yet. I need to type my passport number.
6. ______________ your bag in the overhead compartment.
7. The plane leaves at 6:15. ______________ be late!
8. ______________ us about your trip. Was it fun?

G Write to Speak

Make a list of suggestions using imperatives. Suggest what a friend should do for his or her next trip. Then share your ideas with a partner.

1. ______________________________________.
2. ______________________________________.
3. ______________________________________.
4. ______________________________________.

H Use the Language

Talking to a travel agent

Role-play a conversation between a travel agent and a customer.

Travel Agent: Help your customer book a trip. Answer questions about how he or she can prepare for it.

Customer: Book a trip and ask the travel agent about how to prepare for it.

After you finish, summarize your conversation with another pair.

Check Your Progress

1 Listen to the conversation and choose the correct answer. Track 043

1. Where is Erica?

a. at home with her laptop b. a friend's house c. at a travel agency

2. Who is she talking to?

a. her travel partner b. a man on a plane c. a travel agent

2 Listen again. Put a check mark (✓) next to true or false.

1. There are many seats available on the plane.	☐ true	☐ false
2. Erica is afraid of heights.	☐ true	☐ false
3. The man can't find an aisle seat.	☐ true	☐ false
4. Erica decided not to buy a plane ticket.	☐ true	☐ false
5. Erica can't pay for the ticket today.	☐ true	☐ false

3 Choose the correct answers. Listen and check. Track 044

1. _______. We still need to print the tickets.	a. Close not the window	b. Don't close the window
2. _______. Get a window seat.	a. No get a middle seat	b. Don't get a middle seat
3. We need to leave at 9:30. _______.	a. Don't be late	b. Be not late
4. Have a great trip, and _______.	a. taking care	b. take care
5. _______ your bags in the aisle.	a. Don't to put	b. Don't put

4 Write the correct affirmative or negative imperative form of the verbs.

1. ______________________ (try) to get two seats next to each other.

2. ______________________ (pay) the travel agent yet. I can look for a better deal.

3. ______________________ (close) that window. We need to compare prices.

4. ______________________ (go) to bed early the night before the trip.

5. The plane leaves at 10:00. ______________________ (meet) me at the airport at 8:00.

Unit Review

A A Travel Flyer

Create a travel flyer for a place you want to visit.

The flyer must include:

- the name of the place
- a picture of the place
- things you can do there
- things you need to bring
- how to book the trip online
- how long the trip is
- prices and options
- contact information for the travel agency

B Present Your Flyer

After you create your flyer, present it to a partner. Answer any questions he or she has about the place and the trip. Write the questions below.

____

____

____

____

Share your flyer with the class. Vote on the best one. Consider the following:

- Which flyer has the best design?
- Which flyer has the most detail?
- How clear is the information?

C Reminder

Put a check mark (✓) next to the things you can do.

____________ Find basic information in advertisements

____________ Ask for basic information about travel and buy tickets

____________ Discuss plans with other people (for example, what to do and where to go)

Further Practice

A Listen for Information

Listen and fill in the blanks. Then practice the conversation with a partner. Track 045

Travel Agent: Sunstar ____________ ____________. Can I help you?
Customer: Yes, hello. I want to ____________ a trip somewhere. I'm a ____________-____________, so...
Travel Agent: So, are you interested in an ____________ ____________?
Customer: What's that?
Travel Agent: An exciting tour where you can do things like ____________ mountains, take ____________ along beautiful rivers, ride ____________ in the ____________...
Customer: Wow! That sounds ____________. Do you have any trips to the ____________ of ____________ ____________?
Travel Agent: Yes, we do. But a lot of people want those tickets. You ____________ ____________ book soon.
Customer: Okay, ____________ ____________ my friend tonight to talk about the trip. ____________ ____________ ____________ tomorrow?
Travel Agent: Yes, or ____________ ____________ book online. Our website is very easy to use. ____________ ____________ to include your ____________ number when you book your ticket.
Customer: ____________ ____________ your web address, please.
Travel Agent: It's www.sunstar.com.
Customer: Thank you for your help.
Travel Agent: You're welcome. ____________ ____________.

B Prepare to Speak

Listen again and write down some things you can do on an adventure tour. Then use the Internet to write down more ideas.

Adventure Tours

C Practice Speaking

Find a partner. Role-play a conversation between two friends planning to go on an adventure tour. Discuss these details:

What kinds of things do you want to do? Where do you want to go?
What does your friend think about it? What does he or she want to do on an adventure tour?

D Now Speak

Stand up in front of the class with your partner. Role-play your conversation. After all the pairs finish, discuss these questions:

A. Which pairs were fast? Did they make many mistakes?
B. Which pairs didn't make many mistakes? Were they fast?

MEMO

UNIT 4

Planning for the Future

Scan and find the tracks.

Before You Read

◆ **Talk about these questions with your classmates.**

1. When you were a child, what did you want to be when you grew up?
2. What kind of job do you want now?
3. Why do you want that job?

Vocabulary

◆ **Read the definitions. Then match each word in bold with its definition.**

A. special care or treatment
B. of or relating to cities and the people who live in them
C. to earn a degree or diploma from a school, college, or university
D. a medical doctor
E. money available to a business or person
F. the work of designing and creating roads, bridges, buildings, products, or systems
G. a person who studies something closely to get information from it
H. old; past middle age

1. ______ Some students are stressed about what to do after they **graduate**.

2. ______ The world's population is starting to include more and more **elderly** people.

3. ______ Some people need a lot of medical **attention** when they get older.

4. ______ **Physician** assistant jobs will see a lot of growth in the future.

5. ______ The position of systems **analyst** is highly valued in some companies.

6. ______ **Engineering** is a position that involves a lot of planning and development.

7. ______ Many people are moving from rural areas to **urban** ones.

8. ______ Most businesses need accountants to handle their **finances**.

4A Main Reading

What Will You Do When You Graduate?

Track 046

In college, many students choose a career that will last a lifetime. The thought of finding the right job when they graduate makes some students anxious. The good news for those who are unsure is that a number of jobs will see growth in the future.

Business experts believe that health care will be the best industry for employment. Over half of the world's population will reach old age in the coming years. The elderly require a lot of medical attention. Nurses and physician assistants are both important to health care institutions, and these jobs should see the most growth. In fact, the field of nursing is expected to grow by twenty-three percent. The number of physician

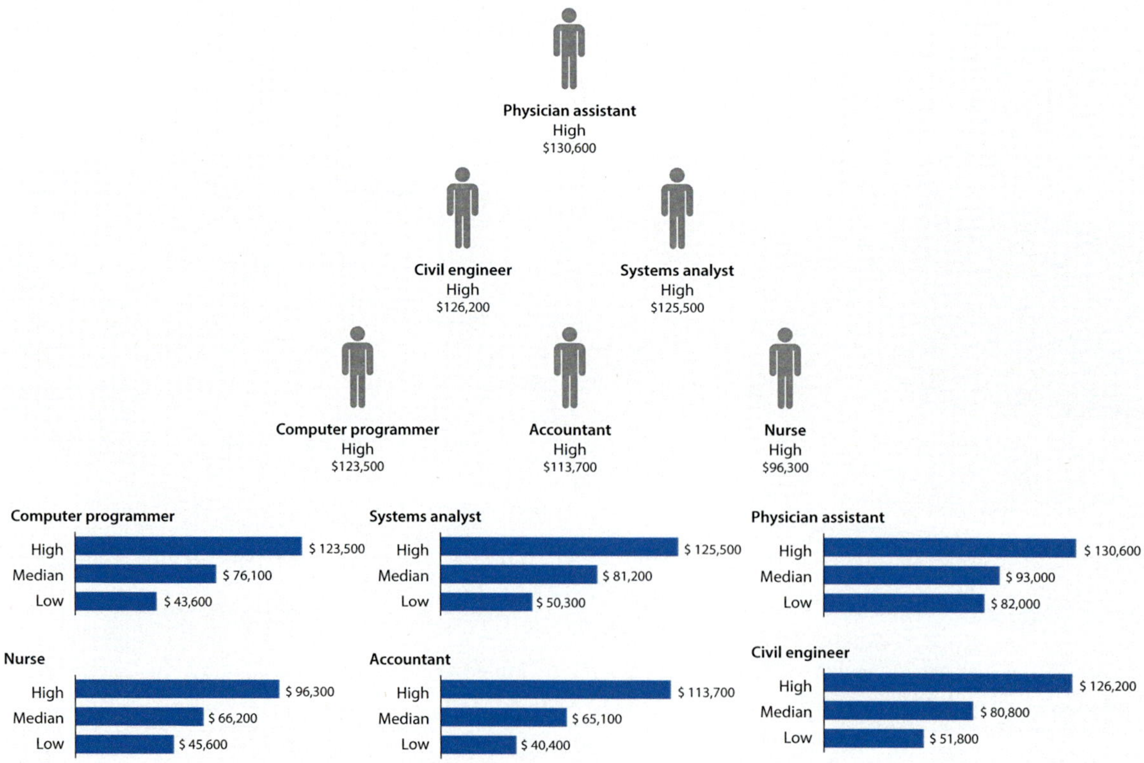

▲ Yearly salaries of select jobs (in US dollars)

assistants will increase by about forty percent.

Another industry that will boom over the next twenty years is the computer industry. Programmers will continue to be in demand. Those with practical experience will be even more valuable to large companies. There is an expected thirty-four percent increase in the number of programmers. The position of systems analyst is also highly valued, and that field should grow by twenty percent.

Other growing areas may not seem as exciting. Civil engineering involves planning transportation and development in urban areas. Urban planning will become even more important as people continue to move from rural areas into urban areas. So civil engineering will grow by about twenty-four percent. Likewise, accounting will remain important. There are few businesses that do not need an accountant to handle their finances. The position is likely to see a twenty-two percent increase in the future.

In an ever-changing job market, many types of jobs are expected to see growth in the future. Selecting from one of the fields that is expected to grow will help you make a decision when it is time to choose a career that is right for you!

Review the Highlights

◆ Mark up the text and infographic according to the instructions.

1. Look at Paragraph 2. Circle the industry that experts believe will need the most workers in the future.
2. Look at Paragraph 2. Circle who will need a lot of medical attention.
3. Look at Paragraph 3. Underline who will be valuable in the computer industry.
4. Look at Paragraph 4. Put a star next to the job that involves development of urban areas.
5. Look at the infographic. Write the job that makes the highest salary of all. ______________
6. Look at the infographic. Write the job that makes the lowest salary of all. ______________

Check Your Comprehension

◆ **Circle the correct answer.**

1. What is the good news for students who graduate? Details: what
   a. There will be more jobs in rural areas.
   b. A number of jobs will see growth.
   c. The world's population will be older.
   d. Programmers will not be in demand.

2. Which field will see the most growth in the future? Details: which
   a. Civil engineering
   b. Accounting
   c. Health care
   d. Computer programming

3. What do companies in the computer industry value? Details: what
   a. Practical experience
   b. Systems analysts
   c. Engineers
   d. The elderly

4. What is NOT true about civil engineering? Negative fact
   a. It will grow by twenty-four percent.
   b. It involves transportation.
   c. It is needed in urban planning.
   d. It is part of the health care industry.

5. What is the purpose of the reading? Purpose
   a. To persuade graduates to go into health care
   b. To help students choose a job for the future
   c. To assist large finance companies
   d. To help students graduate

◆ **Complete the summary. Write the words from the reading that best fit in the blanks. One word is extra.**

urban graduate engineering attention finances elderly physician analysts

Many college students are worried about what career path to take once they 1. ______________. The good news is that a number of fields will see growth in the future. 2. ______________ assistant and nursing positions will both see growth. Jobs in the health care industry are generally a good choice because 3. ______________ people make up a large percentage of the world's population, and they need a lot of medical 4. ______________. The computer industry will also grow. Programmers and systems 5. ______________ will be needed. Civil 6. ______________ jobs will also be in demand. These positions involve transportation and 7. ______________ planning. Although the job market is always changing, there are many career possibilities for college graduates.

Linked Skills Activity

◆ **Read the job descriptions listed below. Can you add anything to them?**

Teacher – helps others learn; ______________________________

Artist – makes art with paint, clay, sculpture, or photography; ______________________________

Baker – bakes cakes, cookies, bread, etc.; ______________________________

Lawyer – helps explain the law to others; ______________________________

Astronomer – studies the stars and space; ______________________________

Architect – designs buildings or houses; ______________________________

Farmer – plants food to grow and sell; ______________________________

Gardener – grows and cares for plants; ______________________________

Dentist – fixes medical problems in people's mouths; ______________________________

◆ **Once you have finalized the descriptions, discuss the jobs with your partner. Make sure to answer the questions below as you talk.**

What kind of training is required to perform each job?
Which jobs would you want to do? Why?
Which jobs would you not want to do? Why?

◆ **Choose one of the topics below and discuss it with your partner.**

1. Why did you choose your major?

2. What would you like to do when you graduate? What is your dream job?

Career Support and Guidance at Keimyung University

Track 047

[KMU Core Competency: Problem Solving Ability]

The Career Services Center and the University Job Plus Center at Keimyung University are committed to supporting students in achieving their career goals. Each semester, hundreds of students, including freshmen, take the first steps toward a successful career by using the resources and expert guidance these centers provide.

One of many services available is one-on-one counseling, where students can discover their strengths, explore their interests, and set clear career objectives. They can also take career and personality tests, such as the MBTI, to learn more about jobs that match their skills, preferences, and future ambitions.

Students can also join many different workshops at the Career Services Center and the University Job Plus Center. At these workshops, students learn practical skills such as writing professional resumes, preparing for interviews, and searching for jobs effectively. They prepare students for the challenges of the modern workplace by helping them develop **problem-solving ability** and learning how to express themselves confidently.

The centers also provide Keimyung university students with various internships and job placements. These opportunities provide real-world experiences and an insight into different working environments. They also help students build confidence, understand workplace expectations, develop teamwork skills, and showcase their abilities to potential employers.

By making use of the resources at Keimyung's career centers, students can prepare for their future careers and face the job market with greater confidence.

Check Your Comprehension

1. What services help students discover their career interests and strengths?

   (A) Group seminars on career planning
   (B) One-on-one counseling and career tests
   (C) Workshops on workplace problem-solving
   (D) Mentoring programs with alumni

2. How do the career centers help students gain experience in the workplace?

   (A) By offering internships and job placements
   (B) By providing part-time campus jobs
   (C) By organizing volunteer programs
   (D) By teaching financial management skills

3. What practical skills do students learn in career workshops?

   (A) Time management and team leadership
   (B) Resume writing and interview preparation
   (C) Public speaking and acting techniques
   (D) Foreign language communication skills

Talk or Write about It

1. What job or career would you like to have in the future?

   ____

   ____

2. In what ways can internships and practical experiences help students get ready for the job market?

   ____

   ____

3. Why is it important for university students to start developing career skills early?

   ____

   ____

4C What Are Your Plans?

A Model Conversation

Listen to the interview. Then read the sentences. Listen again. Are the sentences true (t) or false (f)? Track 048

1. ______ Phillip is thinking of going to college.
2. ______ Phillip is studying computer science.
3. ______ Sonya is working in Spain for six months.
4. ______ Sonya is traveling for six months.
5. ______ Yaser is going to apply to university.
6. ______ Yaser is working on his grandparents' farm.

For the false sentences, why are they false?

Brief note

To "think of" or about something means that you are considering it—that you might do it in the future.

B Vocabulary

Listen to the interview again. Circle the words that you hear.

gap year run volunteer apply student loan experience field nanny

Now write each word next to the correct definition. Check your answers with a partner.

	a year between high school and college to travel, work, or rest		money that is borrowed from a bank to pay for school
	time spent doing something and the skills learned while doing it		to formally ask for something such as a job, usually in writing
	a person who helps parents with childcare		a subject of study or a kind of work
	to be the boss of; to direct or manage		to work/help people for no pay; a person who does this

C Vocabulary Comprehension

Fill in the blanks with the correct words from part B.

1. Sonya is going to take care of children. She is going to work as a(n) ________________.
2. Many students take a year off from studying before they go to college. They take a(n) ________________.
3. Our store needs a new employee. You should ________________ for the job.
4. I want to be a teacher, so I'm working as a volunteer at a school to get some ________________.

D Grammar

Present continuous for future plans

Brief note

Remember that you can also use present continuous to talk about things happening at the moment of speaking. For example: *What **are you doing** right now? I'**m making** breakfast.*

subject	*be*	verb + *-ing* (+ object)	future time phrase
I	am	**starting** college	in September.
He / She / It	is	**visiting** Paris	next week.
You / We / They	are	**meeting** a friend	after school.
more future time phrases	soon, later, tonight, tomorrow, tomorrow morning / afternoon / evening, next Sunday, next weekend, in two hours / days / weeks / months / years		

Brief note

People do not always use time phrases. They use them when they want to be specific. These phrases usually come at the beginning or the end of a sentence.

E Grammar Practice

Read each sentence. Write *P* next to sentences about the present and *F* next to sentences about the future.

1. ______ Please be quiet. I'm working on an assignment.
2. ______ My parents are having dinner at that new restaurant after work.
3. ______ He's doing research on local schools.
4. ______ Ahmed is waiting for the bus to take him home.
5. ______ Sarah and her sister are taking the train to London tomorrow.
6. ______ She is taking a shower at the moment.

Put the words in order to make sentences.

7. is / John / this / in / sister / his / visiting / Istanbul / weekend

   ____.

8. you / Saturday / are / what / doing / next

   ____?

9. boyfriend / next / getting / her / and / Jenny / year / married / are

   ____.

F Use the Language

What are you up to?

Think about your plans for next month. Write them as notes. You don't have to write complete sentences.

My plans...

Talk about your plans with a partner. Ask about your partner's plans. Do you have similar plans? When are you going to do these things? Are you and your partner busy?

When you are finished, talk with another pair about their plans. Then share with the class.

Check Your Progress

1 Circle the correct answers.

1. I'm really busy (next week / right now). I'm working on my homework for tomorrow's English class.
2. She's traveling to China (now / next week) to see her brother. She's packing for the trip tomorrow.
3. (Right now / Tomorrow), Troy is waiting for the next train to take him downtown.
4. What are you doing for dinner (right now / later)? Come over to my place at 7!

2 Look at the pictures and complete the sentences with the correct phrases from the box.

- graduating early
- taking a gap year to travel
- volunteering with kids
- applying for a job
- getting experience in the hotel field

1. Lumina is thinking of ____.

2. Brian is thinking about ____.

3. Ivan is thinking about ____.

4. Solange is thinking of ____.

5. Greg is thinking of ____.

3 Put the words in order to make sentences.

1. as / working / nanny / am / a / I

   ____.

2. Trevor / loan / getting / a / is / student

   ____.

3. me / you / volunteering / about / are / thinking / with

   ____?

4D The Career Center

A Authentic Text: A career flyer

Read the flyer and answer the questions.

Brief note

The word "résumé" is often spelled *resume*. Another way to say *résumé* is *CV* (*curriculum vitae*, a Latin phrase).

Regular Activities

Coffee Time
Mon-Fri: 8:30 – 10:00 a.m.
- Meet new employees of the center

Job Fair
Last Thursday of every month
- Meet local employers looking for workers

Résumé Workshop
Third Wednesday of every month: 1:00 – 4:00 p.m.
- Develop your résumé with help from an expert

Career Center

Are you between the ages of 17 and 35? Looking for employment? Trying to decide what to do with your future? Drop by the Career Center and find out about the options available to you.
At the Career Center, you can:
- Start to think about your future
- Learn about career programs
- Get help with your résumé and practice job interview skills
- Learn about volunteering to help you get experience
- Search the job board
- Make an appointment with a career counselor
- Make new friends

Events this week

Rob Vega
Monday: 2:00 – 4:00 p.m.
- Government training programs

Annika Smith
Wednesday: 4:00 – 6:00 p.m.
- Writing a cover letter

Please register at the front desk.

Contact us
By phone: 204-555-6987 By email: info@cpc.edu Like us on Facebook

Brief note

To drop by means to go to a place for a short time without an appointment.

1. Who can use the Career Center?
2. What happens every weekday morning?
3. How often is there a job fair?
4. When can you learn about writing cover letters?
5. How can you get in touch with the center?

B Vocabulary

Write each green word or phrase from part A next to the correct definition.

1. ____________________ from or around this area
2. ____________________ a meeting with someone at a specific time
3. ____________________ a face-to-face meeting to talk about a job
4. ____________________ a written list of your skills and experience
5. ____________________ to speak or write a message to someone
6. ____________________ an event where many employers meet people looking for jobs
7. ____________________ a letter about your experience
8. ____________________ the group of people who run a city, state, country, etc. and make laws
9. ____________________ work done for pay; a job, or the state of having a job
10. ____________________ a person who knows a lot about a subject

C About You

Discuss the questions with a partner.

1. Do you have a résumé? If you do, what do you have on it? If not, what can you write on one?
2. What are some local jobs or companies that you are interested in? Why?

D Grammar

Simple present vs. present continuous

Brief note

Stative verbs such as *love, own, want,* and *know* are not usually used with present continuous.

	simple present	present continuous
present meaning	things that are generally true; routines and habits	things happening at the time of speaking
examples	He **works** at the library. (He has a job at the library. Is he there right now? We don't know.) She **eats** lunch in the cafeteria. (This is her daily routine—she usually does it.)	He**'s working** right now. (He's at his workplace and doing work.) She**'s eating** lunch in the cafeteria. (It is lunchtime now, and she's eating in the cafeteria.)
time expressions	every day, week, month, morning, afternoon in the morning, afternoon, evening usually, often, never	right now at the moment
future meaning	scheduled actions on a timetable or calendar	plans
examples	My plane **leaves** at 6:45 tomorrow evening. Classes **start** on September 15.	I**'m meeting** Mom at the airport tonight. We**'re seeing** a movie on Friday afternoon.

E Grammar Practice

Fill in the blanks with the correct form of the verbs.

1. My sister ________________ (study) biology at university this year. She wants to become a doctor.
2. I usually ________________ (walk) to school, but today I ________________ (take) the bus because I ________________ (be) late.
3. The teacher ________________ (know) all of her students' names.
4. I ________________ (eat) breakfast every morning—I ________________ (need) it so I'm not hungry in class.

F Write to Speak

1. Write five questions you can ask someone about future plans. Use the time expressions below to help you.

next year after school	when you were a child when you graduate	next week in five years

2. Now interview a partner about his or her future plans.

G Use the Language

Career counseling

With your partner, on a separate piece of paper, write a conversation between a career counselor and a person thinking about a new job. Talk about the person's experience, education, and skills. Try to decide on a good career for him or her. Then perform your conversation for the class.

Check Your Progress

1 **Listen to the announcement at the career center and put a check mark (✓) next to the services they offer.** Track 049

job board		volunteer jobs		help with interviews		intern information	
résumé writing		study space		personal problems		cooking lessons	

2 **Listen again and match the two columns to make sentences.**

1. Many students are •
2. Students can drop by •
3. Expert counselors have great advice •
4. Next Friday, ten employers •
5. The job fair is a good way to •
6. Students should •

- • **a.** thinking about employment options.
- • **b.** sign up early for the job fair.
- • **c.** meet people from local companies.
- • **d.** are visiting the SCCC.
- • **e.** the career center or make an appointment.
- • **f.** about interview skills and résumés.

3 **Circle the correct form of the verb according to the description.**

1. David (lives / is living) on the south side of London. — generally true
2. I (take / am taking) accounting next semester. — plan
3. They usually (study / are studying) in the library. — routine
4. I (go / am going) to see a movie tomorrow. — plan
5. He (has / is having) an interview tomorrow at 4:00. — scheduled action

4 **Fill in the blanks with the correct words from the box.**

appointment	employment	local	need	studying
get in touch	résumé	end	interview	cover letter

Sean: I ______________ to find a way to pay for school next year.

Counselor: Well, let's think about your options, Sean. What are you ______________?

Sean: I'm in my first year of the engineering program.

Counselor: Okay. Are you looking for ______________ right now?

Sean: Not now, but classes ______________ for the summer next month. I'm thinking about getting a summer job close to campus—someplace ______________.

Counselor: We can work on writing your ______________ and ______________ ______________ together.

Sean: That's a good idea. I'm also thinking of practicing my ______________ skills.

Counselor: That's a great idea, too.

Sean: Can I make a(n) ______________ for next week?

Counselor: Sure. Let's say next Tuesday at 3:00. Here's my card. You can always ______________ ______________ ______________ with me by e-mail or phone.

4E Making Decisions

A Model Conversation

Read the conversation. Then listen. Track 050

Elisa: Hey, Malak. You look really **worried**! What's the matter?
Malak: I decided to go to college next year, but I don't know what major to choose.
Elisa: Oh, that's a **tough** one. What do you like to do?
Malak: Well, I really enjoy being **outdoors**. I don't want an office job because I **can't stand** sitting down all day. But my parents think I should study **IT**. That's why I'm stressed.
Elisa: Hmm. I can understand that. But your parents can't make this kind of **decision** for you. What other things do you like doing?
Malak: I'm not sure. I need to think about that because my parents want to discuss my decision this week.
Elisa: The **recreation leader** program at the local college might be interesting. What do you think about that?
Malak: Sounds cool. I'll **look into** it. Thanks, Elisa.

Brief note

"IT" is an abbreviation of the phrase *information technology*.

B Vocabulary

Write each bold word or phrase from part A next to the correct definition.

1. ______________ hard
2. ______________ outside
3. ______________ to hate
4. ______________ someone who leads activity groups (arts, sports, games, etc.)
5. ______________ what a person chose; a choice
6. ______________ thinking about problems and feeling stressed
7. ______________ to try to get information about something
8. ______________ the study of computers and how to use them to keep and communicate information

C Vocabulary: Showing interest and understanding

Read the following expressions and their meanings.

a. What's the matter?	*What's wrong?*
b. That's a tough one.	*That's a hard problem.*
c. I (can) understand that.	*I see why you feel that way.*

Now listen to three people talk. Which expression should you use in each situation? Write the letter. Track 051

1. __________ **2.** __________ **3.** __________

D Grammar

Gerunds and infinitives; conjunction *because*

verbs followed by gerunds (verb + *-ing*)	verbs followed by infinitives (*to* + verb)	verbs followed by both
enjoy finish quit dislike practice	learn need promise want decide	hate like love can't stand
I **enjoy** play**ing** piano. He **loves** listen**ing** to music.	She is **learn**ing **to swim**. We **want to go** downtown.	I **love to watch** TV in the morning. I **love listening** to the radio at night.

using *because* to give a reason	
because **clause, clause** *(comma needed)*	**Because** I like to watch TV at night, I often stay up too late.
clause + ***because*** **clause** *(no comma needed)*	I often stay up too late **because** I like to watch TV at night.

Brief note

A *clause* is a group of words with a subject and a verb.

E Grammar Practice

Find the errors in the sentences. Then rewrite them correctly. One sentence has two errors.

1. I enjoy to study English, because it will help me in the future.

____

2. She promised going shopping with me on the weekend.

____

3. My friend learned speak English by watching TV.

____

4. Because my brother can't play violin, we can't stand listen to him practice.

____

F Use the Language

What should they study?

Interview three of your classmates. Ask them about their hobbies and interests. Then suggest college majors for them. Fill in the chart with the information. (Note: If you have a major, don't say it. If you know a person's major, suggest a second major.) When you are finished, discuss your ideas with each person. What do they think about your suggestions? Share your results with the class.

Person	Hobbies/Interests	Major

Check Your Progress

1 Complete the crossword.

Across →

4. *IT* means "information ______."
6. The recreation ______ is teaching us a new game.
7. not inside

Down ↓

1. I can't ______ football. It's so boring!
2. To make a ______ is to *choose*.
3. stressed
4. hard
5. Do you prefer ______ in stores or online?
6. I want to know more about this major. I'll ______ into it.

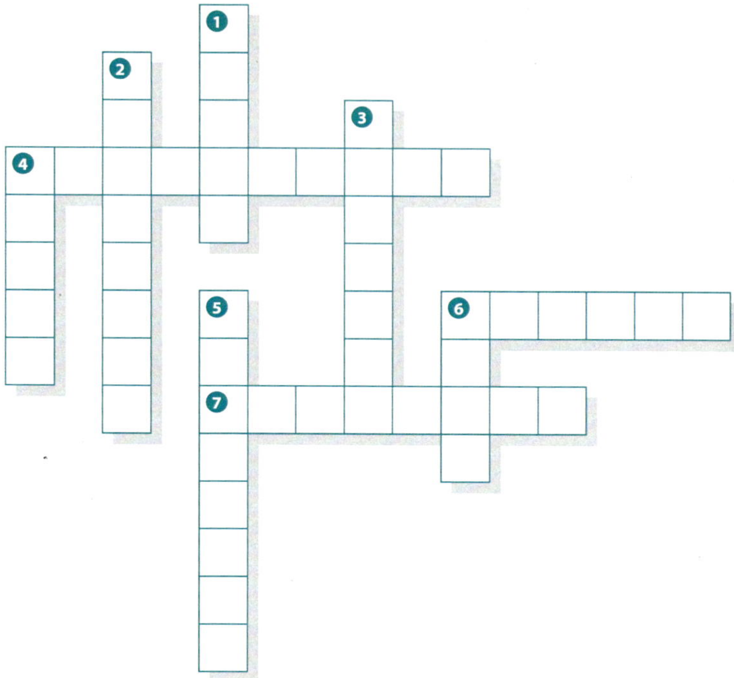

2 Choose the correct answers.

1. Cheryl hates ____________ carrot soup.
   a. eating b. to eat c. both a and b
2. Mr. and Mrs. Roberts need ____________ their house.
   a. selling b. to sell c. both a and b
3. Do you still practice ____________ piano every day?
   a. playing b. to play c. both a and b
4. Kamal loves ____________ at the hospital each week.
   a. volunteering b. to volunteer c. both a and b
5. My sister quit ____________ at the restaurant today.
   a. working b. to work c. both a and b
6. You need ____________ your classes before September.
   a. choosing b. to choose c. both a and b

3 Listen to the sentences. Put a check mark (✓) next to the ones with a pause. Then add a comma (,) where you hear the pause. Track 052

1. She's studying IT because she's really interested in computers. ☐
2. Because Mary can't decide on a major she feels stressed. ☐
3. Most of my friends hate learning math because it's very confusing. ☐
4. Because he dislikes working outside Rob isn't studying agriculture. ☐
5. Because Natalia loves acting she works in the entertainment field. ☐

4F Deciding on the Future

A Model Conversation

Read the conversation. Then listen. Track 053

Ahmed: Laura, congratulations! I heard you're going to medical school.
Laura: Thanks. Yeah, I found out yesterday.
Ahmed: Well, I'll call you when I'm sick.
Laura: I'll be a student for a long time. For the near future, you'll need to find another doctor.
Ahmed: You'll be great. I'm really happy for you. But I don't think I'll tell my mom about it.
Laura: Why not?
Ahmed: She'll be upset. She wants me to be a doctor, but I want to be a chef. I think I want to go to culinary school.
Laura: Do you know any good restaurants, then? Let's have dinner to celebrate.

B Vocabulary

Listen to the words. Mark the stress in each word. Then practice saying them with a partner. Track 054

architect – architecture	doctor – medicine	teacher – education
actor – theater arts	chef – culinary arts	carpenter – carpentry

Now say a sentence about each type of person and their field.

For example: *An **architect** works in the field of **architecture**.*

C Grammar

Brief note

In conversation, use the contracted form of *will* (*he'll, you'll, etc.*) and the negative form of *will not* (*I won't,* not *I'll not*).

Future with *will*

using *will* to express future time: *will* + base verb	
possibilities	It's cloudy. I think it **will rain** this afternoon.
offers	The phone is ringing. I'**ll answer** it.
decisions made when speaking	That looks like a nice place to visit. Maybe we'**ll go** there next month.

want / would like + object + infinitive

expressing preferences with *want / would like*	
with a noun phrase	*Less formal*: I **want** a cup of coffee. *More formal*: I **would like** / I'**d like** a cup of coffee (please).
with an infinitive	*Less formal*: I **want** to see a movie tonight. *More formal*: I **would like** / I'**d like** to see a movie tonight.
with an object + infinitive	*Less formal*: My mother **wants** me to go medical school. *More formal*: I'**d like** you to help me with my résumé.

D Grammar Practice

Read the sentences with *will*. How is it used? Write *P* for a possibility, *O* for an offer, or *D* for a decision made when speaking.

1. ______ Please sit down. I'll bring you some water.
2. ______ That restaurant looks good. I'll book a table there tomorrow.
3. ______ The sky is very dark. I think it will rain this afternoon.
4. ______ That movie is really funny. You'll like it.
5. ______ That bag looks heavy. I'll carry it for you.
6. ______ That car is too expensive. Nobody will buy it.

Underline the errors and write the correct word(s) in the blank.

7. I'd like to eggs for breakfast, please. ______________
8. My brother wants his friend helps him with his car. ______________
9. She want to study film and television at college. ______________
10. I'd would like my husband to cook dinner for me this weekend. ______________

E Use the Language

Talking about people's plans

Choose one picture. Think about the person in it and write a few sentences about his or her plans and future dreams. What does the person want to do? What do you think he or she will do?

Read your sentences to a partner. He or she will try to guess which picture you're describing. Ask your partner why he or she thinks this. Is your partner correct?

Check Your Progress

1 **Read the following ad. Guess which words go in the blanks, and write your guesses on the lines.**

Bayside Vocational College

1. _____ you like to begin an interesting new career? Bayside Vocational College would like 2. _____ help you reach your professional goals! Here are just a few of our programs:

- 3. _____ Arts: Restaurants and hotels are always looking for employees with good cooking skills.
- 4. _____: Learn about building, and even learn to make beautiful wood furniture.
- 5. _____: Learn to teach young children and get ready for a job in childcare.

Our teachers have many years of experience in these fields, and they 6. _____ their students to be successful!

Join us for a presentation on Thursday, May 12 from 2:00 – 4:00 p.m. We 7. _____ answer your questions and help you prepare for your future!

At BCT, we 8. _____ our students to reach their dreams!

www.bct.com

Brief note

A *vocational* school or college teaches skills for specific jobs.

1. ____________________

2. ____________________

3. ____________________

4. ____________________

5. ____________________

6. ____________________

7. ____________________

8. ____________________

2 **Now listen to the ad and check your answers above.** Track 055

3 **Match the questions and answers.**

1. Are you still thinking about becoming an actor?

2. What would you like your son to do?

3. Would Jasmine like to continue studying architecture next year?

4. Does your professor want you to think about medicine?

5. Why doesn't Sam want to be a carpenter?

a. I really want John to work in the education field.

b. Because he doesn't think he will earn enough money.

c. Yes, I still really want to work in the theater.

d. No, she's going to change her major.

e. Yes, Dr. Song really wants me to be a doctor one day!

4 **Underline the errors and rewrite the sentences correctly.**

1. I will dropped you off at the university.

____.

2. The exam tomorrow won't easy.

____.

3. Your bags look heavy—I'll helping you.

____.

4. That coffee smells good. Maybe I have some.

____.

4G Ready for a Break

A Model Monologues

Read the conversation. Then listen. Track 056

Marco: Hi, Sophie. What's the matter? Why do you look upset?

Sophie: I'm not upset. I'm just tired of looking at these brochures from different colleges. I have to decide soon, so I'm researching a lot of schools and programs.

Marco: I'm ready for a break, too. I just finished cleaning up my house. I was dog-sitting for a friend, so there was hair everywhere! I'm tired of scrubbing and vacuuming. Let's get some coffee and complain.

Sophie: Coffee sounds great. I'll meet you at the coffee shop in half an hour.

Marco: All right, I'll see you then.

Listen to the conversation again. What is Sophie tired of?

____

> **Brief note**
> The phrase "tired of" + noun/gerund means that you are bored or annoyed about something. You want to stop doing it.

B Vocabulary

Match the words with the correct definitions.

1. vacuum	**a.** a rest or a vacation from work or school
2. iron	**b.** to get information about something
3. scrub	**c.** to care for someone else's dog for a short time
4. bake	**d.** a small, thin book or magazine with pictures and information about a place, a business, etc.
5. brochure	**e.** to smooth out wrinkles in clothes using a heated appliance
6. break	**f.** to clean using a machine that sucks up dirt and dust
7. dog-sit	**g.** to cook food, especially in an oven, using dry heat
8. research	**h.** to clean something by rubbing it hard with a brush or cloth

C In Your World

What are three things you're tired of doing? Why? Ask a partner. Suggest what he or she can do instead.

> **Brief note**
> *Instead of..., you can...* is used to suggest a different action. For example: *Instead of doing the laundry, you can take your clothes to the dry cleaners.*

D Grammar

Questions with *why* and answers; conjunction *so*

asking for reasons with *why*	
question	**answer**
Why are you going to college?	**Because** I want to get a good job. I'm going to college **because** I want to get a good job.
	To get a good job. / I'm going to college **to get** a good job.

using *so*	
to give a reason	I'm going to college **so** (**that**) I can get a good job. Hugo gets up early in the morning **so** (**that**) he is not late for work.
to state a result	Kim was really late for work, **so** her boss got angry. I'm tired of studying, **so** I'm taking a short break.

Brief note

You can use *so that* to answer *why* questions, or you can use *so* without *that*.

E Grammar Practice

Write complete questions. Then answer them using *so*.

1. Q: Why / you / come / this school? → ____________________?

A: ____________________

2. Q: Why / you / want / study / English? → ____________________?

A: ____________________

3. Q: Why / people / want / learn / new languages? → ____________________?

A: ____________________

F Listen to Speak

Listen to the conversation and answer the questions. Track 057

1. What is Jared tired of? ____________________

2. What does Fatima suggest he do instead? ____________________

G Use the Language

Let's take a break!

Work with a partner. Take turns being Student A and Student B.

Student A

You are in your final year of school. You want to take a semester off, and you want your friend to take the semester off with you so that you can travel together. Explain to your friend why you want to take a break.

Student B

Your friend wants to take a semester off from school and wants you to take a break, too. You think this is a really bad idea, and you want your friend to stay in school and finish his or her studies. Tell your friend why taking a break is a bad idea.

Check Your Progress

1 Put the words in order to make sentences.

1. _____ floor / you / of / are / scrubbing / tired / the _______________?
2. _____ tired / baking / of / I'm _______________!
3. _____ taking / ironing / instead / I'm / break / of / a _______________.

2 Choose the correct answers.

1. **Robin:** Why are you still here?
   Ted: I'm waiting for Junko so _____.
   a. she can give me a ride home
   b. I forgot money for the bus ride
2. **Mr. Moyer:** Why do you want to go to college?
   Jill: I love helping sick people, so _____.
   a. I'd like to be a doctor
   b. I will make a high salary
3. **Aunt Mia:** Why are you sitting down?
   Tonya: _____, so I'm not doing it anymore.
   a. I love cleaning the house
   b. I'm tired of cleaning the house

3 Read the email and answer the questions. Write complete sentences.

Dear Mom and Dad,

Brandon and I are doing well here in New York. I can't believe I'm living with my little brother in a tiny apartment! Because Brandon doesn't like to cook, do the dishes, or vacuum, I do most of the work at home. I hate that! And sometimes I'm tired of hanging out with him so much, so I go to my room and close the door to take a break.

But there are some good things about living together. When people ask me "Why are you living with your little brother?" I usually tell them it's so that we can save money. But also, Brandon and I will never be alone in the big city! I'll always have him, and he'll always have me.

I'll write more later.

Love,
Lucy

1. Why does Lucy do most of the housework?

   _______________.

2. Why does Lucy go to her room and close the door?

   _______________.

3. Why do Lucy and Brandon live together? (Give two reasons.)

   ____

   _______________.

Unit Review

A A Radio Announcement

Listen to an announcement on a college radio station. Fill in the blanks with the missing information. Track 058

- The ad is about ________________.
- Only ________________% of students use the college's Career Center.
- The Career Center is open from ________________ to ________________, six days a week.
- Volunteers can help with ________________ and ________________.

B Write to Speak

What are some questions you might ask a career counselor? Write them down.

____

____

____

____

C Career Counseling

Work with a partner. One of you will play a career counselor, and the other will play a student.

Career Counselor

You work in the Career Center at a large university. A student comes to you to discuss career options. Talk with the student. Find out what he or she is interested in. Then give the student some advice. Suggest at least two career options.

Student

You're a student at a large university. You go to see a career counselor to discuss your plans for the future. You don't know what you want to do, but your parents want you to be a teacher. You don't want to be a teacher. Ask the counselor for advice.

D Reminder

Put a check mark (✓) next to the things you can do.

________________ Start a conversation

________________ Discuss plans with other people

________________ Briefly explain and give reasons for actions and plans if you have time to prepare

Further Practice

A Read to Write

Read the paragraph.

I'm finishing college soon. When I think about my future, two things are very important to me. The first is getting the right kind of job. I love art! I'm studying art history so that I can work in a museum. I want to keep studying art and help others learn about it. Second, I like helping people. I volunteer at a hospital, playing with sick kids and reading to them. I don't care about making a lot of money, so I don't want to work all the time. I'd like to have a lot of free time so that I can continue volunteering in the future.

B Prewrite

What's important to you?

When people make decisions about the future, they consider many different things. What is most important to you when you're making plans for the future? Read the list and add one item. Then number the items from 1 (very important) to 9 (not important).

_____ money

_____ time with family and friends

_____ becoming a better person

_____ being creative

_____ meeting new people

_____ helping people

_____ doing exciting things

_____ traveling

_____ education / learning new things

_____ ______________________________ (your idea)

C Write to Speak

Write a few sentences describing what is important to you as you plan your future, what's not important, and why.

____

____

____

____

D Now Speak

Ask your partner what is most important to him or her when deciding a career. When you answer, do not read from your answers above. Compare your partner's answers to yours. Which are the same? Which are different? Give reasons for your decisions.

Then work together to create a new list. Compare the new list to the old lists. What changed?

MEMO

UNIT 5 Free Time Activities

Scan and find the tracks.

Before You Read

◆ **Talk about these questions with your classmates.**

1. What kinds of exercises do you usually do?
   How often do you do them?
2. Do you think walking is a good way to exercise? Why or why not?
3. How far do you think a person would go if they took ten thousand steps?

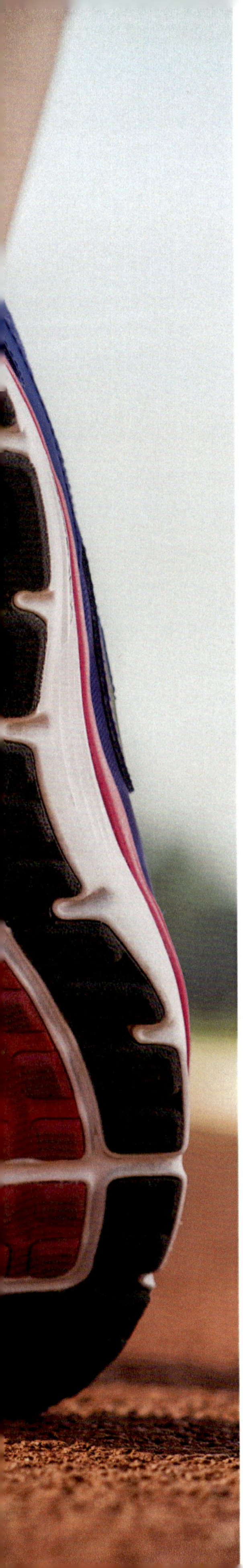

Vocabulary

◆ **Read the definitions. Then match each word in bold with its definition.**

A. the smallest amount possible; not less than
B. of a medium or typical amount
C. a goal; what a person wants to do or achieve
D. done in a usual, relaxed way
E. a measure of energy used by humans and animals
F. the amount of strength, energy, or focus given to an activity
G. a period of time used for an activity
H. to put effort into reaching a goal
I. speed; how fast something or someone moves
J. to focus one's eyes and thoughts on something

1. ______ One thirty-minute exercise **session** per day results in health benefits.
2. ______ People should exercise **at least** five times per week.
3. ______ The **target** of exercise should be to increase the heart rate for ten minutes.
4. ______ Walking at a fast **pace** for ten minutes three times a day is good exercise.
5. ______ **Casual**, slow walking does not really work the heart.
6. ______ Many people **invest** time and effort in their health.
7. ______ When you exercise, **pay attention** to your breathing.
8. ______ A person with an inactive lifestyle does not burn many **calories** per day.
9. ______ Health benefits result from a **moderate** amount of daily exercise.
10. ______ A high-**intensity** workout will make you sweat a lot.

Walking Is Not Enough

Track 059

All of us need to exercise. However, not everyone has the time or desire to join a gym. Everyone can walk, though! But how can a person with an inactive lifestyle walk for exercise? The key is to set an attainable goal. Just by doing daily chores, an inactive person probably already takes around two thousand steps per day. For exercise purposes, the aim should then be to walk more over time. A popular exercise goal for people these days is ten thousand steps per day.

Reaching a certain number of steps is not enough, however. Casual, slow walking does not really exercise the heart. It does not burn many calories, either. Health benefits result from at least thirty minutes of daily moderate-intensity exercise.

The intensity of a workout only needs to be enough to increase a person's heart

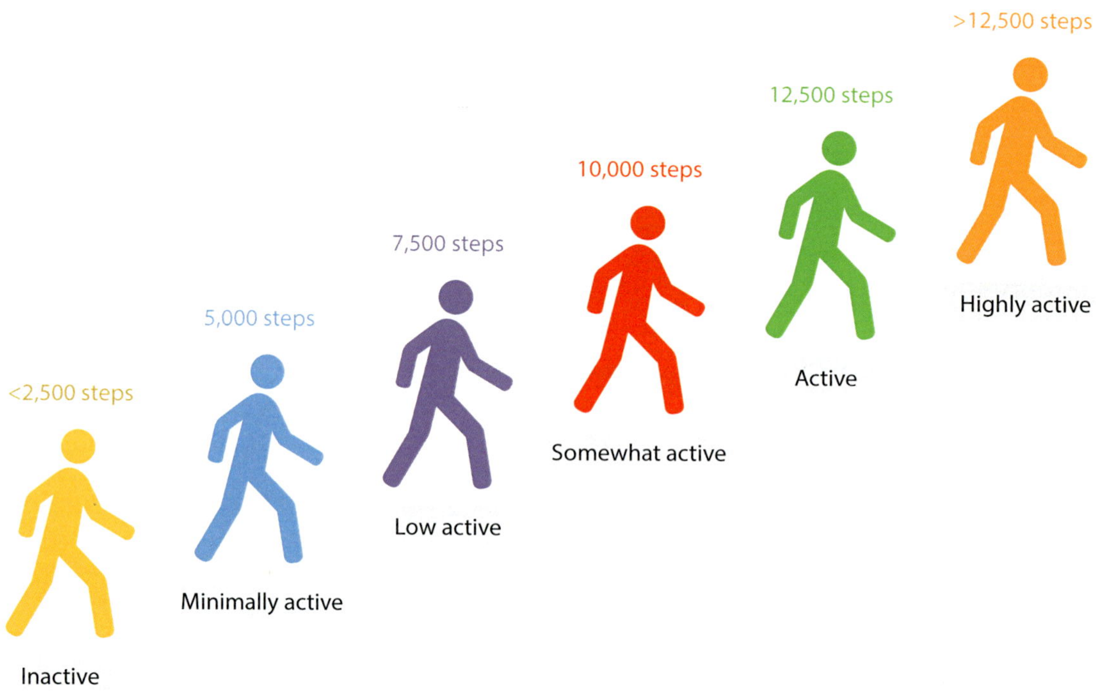

▲ What kind of walker are you?

rate. Simply walking fast can do that. Keep in mind, though, that such fast walking needs to continue for at least ten minutes. Five minutes of fast walking six times a day will not benefit one's health. Three 10-minute sessions can total thirty minutes per day. And that daily goal should be met five times per week.

Dr. Vicki Harber is a researcher at the University of Alberta in Canada. She says, "People might think that the number of steps is most important. They may not pay much attention to the pace or effort invested in taking those steps." With a ten-thousand step daily target, Harber recommends that about one-third of those daily steps should be at a faster pace.

Review the Highlights

◆ **Mark up the text and infographic according to the instructions.**

1. Look at Paragraph 1. Underline the number of steps that an inactive person takes per day.
2. Look at Paragraph 1. Underline the number of steps that are a popular goal for exercise.
3. Look at Paragraph 2. Circle two problems with casual walking.
4. Look at Paragraph 3. Underline three things that a workout should be or do.
5. Look at the infographic. Circle the type of walker who walks ten thousand steps per day.

Check Your Comprehension

◆ **Circle the correct answer.**

1. What is the main idea of the reading? Main idea
   a. Chores make people walk.
   b. Ten thousand steps is not much.
   c. Walking fast is good exercise.
   d. Walking is bad exercise.

2. Why does the writer mention ten thousand steps? Purpose
   a. As a common goal
   b. As a minimum amount
   c. As a cause of health problems
   d. As part of an experiment

3. Which exercise does the writer say can increase a person's heart rate? Details: what
   a. Ten minutes of chores
   b. Five-minute gym workouts
   c. Casual walking
   d. Fast walking

4. What is NOT true about a good daily workout? Negative fact
   a. If it is intense, five minutes is enough.
   b. It should happen five times a week.
   c. It should increase a person's heart rate.
   d. The total time should be thirty minutes a day.

5. Which statement is supported by the infographic? Inference
   a. Active people walk between nine thousand and ten thousand steps per day.
   b. Inactive people do not walk at all during the day.
   c. Low-active people walk more than minimally-active people.
   d. Walking more than twelve thousand steps per day is not an attainable goal.

◆ **Complete the summary. Write the words from the reading that best fit in the blanks. One word is extra.**

pace calories casual at least target invest pay attention session

Not everyone likes going to the gym, but simply walking at a fast 1. ___________ can increase a person's heart rate and benefit one's health. Walking can be a good daily workout if it is done for a long enough 2. ___________ of time and at the right pace. Ten thousand steps per day is a popular 3. ___________ these days. This is an attainable goal even for only somewhat active people. People need to 4. ___________ to more than just the number of steps they take, though. Walking at a(n) 5. ___________ pace does not increase one's heart rate or burn many 6. ___________. The key is to aim for a workout of moderate intensity for 7. ___________ thirty minutes five times per week.

Linked Skills Activity

◆ **Read the following list of chores or activities that people normally do. How many calories do you think each activity burns when a person does it for thirty minutes? Rank these chores and activities in order from 1 (burns the most calories) to 10 (burns the least calories). Then compare your ranking with a partner.**

Rank	Calories Burned	Rank	Calories Burned
_____ cleaning the house	( )	_____ ironing clothes	( )
_____ cooking	( )	_____ making beds	( )
_____ doing dishes by hand	( )	_____ shopping	( )
_____ doing yard work	( )	_____ sweeping	( )
_____ folding clothes	( )	_____ watching TV	( )

◆ **Read the information below and calculate how many calories each chore actually burns in thirty minutes. Write your calculations in the chart above.**

Watching TV does not burn many calories, but it does burn some. When watching thirty minutes of your favorite show on TV, you can burn about thirty calories. Looking to burn some extra calories around the house? Try cooking, ironing, or folding clothes for thirty minutes. All three of those chores will burn about twice as many calories as watching TV. Cleaning the house or sweeping are even better. By doing those for thirty minutes, you could burn ten to fifteen more calories than cooking. Shopping isn't bad exercise, either. Doing that for thirty minutes burns three times as many calories as watching TV. Are there lots of beds in your home? Making beds for thirty minutes will burn four times the calories of watching TV. Doing dishes by hand burns five times as many. The best chore to burn calories is yard work. In thirty minutes, that burns about two hundred calories.

◆ **Look at the list of chores above. With a partner, talk about two of the chores. What actions performed while doing those chores burn calories? Write your ideas below. Share your ideas with the class.**

Chore	Process
#1: ______________	______________________________
#2: ______________	______________________________

Tradition Meets Modern Life at Keimyung University

Track 060

[KMU Core Competency: Comprehensive Thinking]

Keimyung University's Daemyung Campus, located in Nam-gu, Daegu, is famous across Korea for its beauty. The red brick buildings, covered with ivy vines, create a unique and elegant atmosphere. Together with Seongseo Campus, it has been a popular filming location since the 1990s, appearing in over 100 movies, TV dramas, and commercials. Its charm continues to attract both visitors and filmmakers, making it one of the most special places at Keimyung University.

One of the most impressive places on Seongseo Campus is the Keimyung Art Center, the top performance hall in Daegu and Gyeongbuk. It has modern facilities for performances like musicals, operas, plays, and dances. The center also has 1,954 seats, which represent the year 1954, when Daemyung Campus was founded. Many students and visitors admire this venue for its size and cultural importance, and it continues to be a proud symbol of Keimyung University's dedication to the arts.

Another highlight is Keimyung Hanhakchon, a site that preserves Korea's traditional housing culture. It includes Keimyung Seodang, a traditional building named Kyejunghun, and a peaceful garden. These areas contrast beautifully with the Western-style architecture on campus, creating a mix of old and new. In 2015, the Korean president and world leaders visited this site during the World Water Forum, showing its cultural significance.

Visiting Keimyung's campuses encourages **comprehensive thinking** by helping students understand the connection between tradition and modern life. These attractions are perfect for relaxing, reflecting, and finding inspiration during free time.

Check Your Comprehension

1. How many movies, dramas, and commercials have been filmed on Daemyung and Seongseo Campuses?
   (A) 30
   (B) 60
   (C) 80
   (D) Over 100

2. What does the number of seats at the Keimyung Art Center represent?
   (A) The year the Daemyung Campus was founded
   (B) The year the Korean War ended
   (C) The number of performances held each year
   (D) The size of the performance hall

3. Who did NOT visit Keimyung Hanhakchon in 2015?
   (A) The Korean President
   (B) World leaders
   (C) A veterinarian
   (D) None of the above

Talk or Write about It

1. How does the campus affect students' college life?

   ____

   ____

2. How do performance facilities, like the Keimyung Art Center, affect the cultural life of local residents?

   ____

   ____

3. Why do you think it is important to preserve traditions?

   ____

   ____

I'll Go Out Tonight

5C Visiting Relatives

A Model Conversation

Read the conversation. Then listen. Track 061

Brief note

"Thanksgiving" is a US holiday in late November. Families get together to eat a big meal, usually including turkey.

Craig: Hi, Sandra. Happy Thanksgiving.
Sandra: You, too! Are you and Marie on your way?
Craig: No, Marie and the kids are still getting ready. I'm calling to say we'll be a little late.
Sandra: That's okay. Actually, I still have a lot of work to do for dinner. I'm running late, too, because I'm chatting online with my grandchildren in California.
Craig: Oh, how *are* they? And their parents? I miss them.
Sandra: Fantastic. The kids are going to visit next month for a week, so we can look forward to that.
Craig: Great! Nina and John are my only niece and nephew, but I hardly ever see them. Hey, maybe I'll take them to a football game.
Sandra: Yes, they'll love that. So, anyway, what time will you get here?
Craig: We'll be there at about 4:30. Want us to bring anything?
Sandra: No, that's all right. Just be ready to eat a lot.
Craig: We're looking forward to the turkey. I always tell everyone about my mother-in-law's great cooking.

Brief note

A person's "mother-in-law" is the mother of his or her spouse. The word *in-law* can be used with other family words, too. For example, your spouse's brother or your sibling's husband is your *brother-in-law*.

B Vocabulary: The US school system

Look at the family tree. Then fill in the blanks with the correct words from the box.

niece	mother-in-law	nephew	grandchildren (*sing.* grandchild)

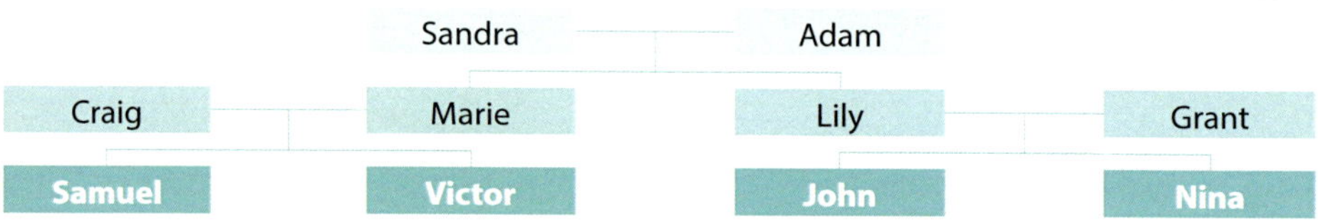

1. Sandra is Craig's ____________________.
2. Sandra and her husband have four ____________________.
3. Nina is Craig and Marie's ____________________.
4. Craig and Marie have a ____________________ named John.

Match the words and phrases with the correct definitions.

5. be on (one's) way •
6. look forward to (something) •
7. run late •
8. miss •

• **a.** to think about (a future event) in a happy way
• **b.** to feel sad because someone isn't with you
• **c.** to be late getting ready; to be behind schedule
• **d.** to be going or traveling somewhere

C Pronunciation

Tell a partner about your relatives.

1. Do you have any brothers-in-law or sisters-in-law? What are they like?
2. How many nieces and nephews do your parents have? How many grandchildren? Do they visit your parents often?
3. What do you do when you visit your relatives?

D Grammar

Future tense

<table>
<tr><th colspan="2">future tense with will and be going to</th></tr>
<tr><td colspan="2">We can speak about the future using will or be going to. Often, you can use either will or be going to:
We'll be a little late. We're going to be a little late.</td></tr>
<tr><th>will</th><th>be going to</th></tr>
<tr><td>With if (first conditional):
If you're late again, mom will be upset.</td><td rowspan="2">For decisions and definite plans made before speaking:
I've packed my suitcase. I'm going to leave soon.
Often, the present continuous has the same meaning:
I've packed my suitcase. I'm leaving soon.</td></tr>
<tr><td>For offers to do something:
Those bags look heavy. I'll help you.</td></tr>
</table>

E Grammar Practice

Circle the correct answers.

1. (We're going to / We'll) sell our car. We put an ad in the newspaper.
2. I think maybe (I'm going to / I'll) cook Thanksgiving dinner this year.
3. If you don't study now, you (aren't / won't be) ready for the final exam.
4. They bought a new house in Texas. They (are going to / will) move in July.
5. A: I'm running late for class, and I still have to take the dog for a walk.
   B: No, go to class. (I'll / I'm going to) take him.

F Read to Write

1. Read the email about a family get-together. Underline the future tense verbs.

> Hey, Lucas.
>
> Thanks for inviting me to visit this weekend, but I won't be able to come. Saturday is my sister's 25th birthday, and we're going to give her a big party. It was my future brother-in-law's idea. He and my sister are going to get married in June. On Saturday, we're going to have dinner at her favorite restaurant and then go to her apartment to have cake and hang out. (I'm going to make the cake!) Maybe we'll play some games. It'll be fun. My aunts, uncles, nieces, and nephews will be there. I'm looking forward to it because I don't see them very often. Anyway, let's get together soon. I'll call you.
>
> Alicia

2. Now look at the pictures below. What kind of family get-together would you like to have this weekend? Choose one. Who will come? What will you do? On a separate sheet of paper, write an email to a friend like the one above.

A barbecue at home

A hiking and/or camping trip

A day at the beach

Check Your Progress

1 **Look at the family tree. Then fill out the list below.**

My niece: ______________________________

My nephew: ______________________________

My children: ______________________________

My parents: ______________________________

Walt's father-in-law: ______________________________

2 **Put the words in order make sentences.**

1. to / bank / the / I / will / go ______________________________.

2. Ian / sister / visit / to / his / going / is ______________________________.

3. spend / grandchildren / Frank / will / his / with / Christmas ______________________________.

4. tonight / Sandra / going / cook / dinner / is / to ______________________________.

5. busy / since / Ben / take / I'll / to / you're / school ______________________________.

3 **David has lots of plans for tomorrow. Write complete sentences about what David will do using *will* or *to be going to*.**

Plans

- visit dentist
- call mother
- buy flowers for wife
- wash car

____

____

____

____

5D Blind Date

A Authentic Text: Online advice column

Read the online advice column. Then discuss the advice with a partner. Do you have any other advice for Stressed Out?

Ask Ms. Trudy

Dear Ms. Trudy,
I'm going on a blind date this Friday night. We're going to have a typical dinner-and-movie date, and maybe we'll go to a café. The guy is my best friend's coworker, and she says he's perfect for me. We're both from Australia, and we are studying in the US right now. Also, we have the same major, business, and the same hobby, photography. But it's my first blind date. I'm a little shy with new people. Maybe I won't like him, or he won't like me. I can't stop worrying about it. I might cancel. What's your advice? Help!
- Stressed Out

Dear Stressed Out,
You shouldn't cancel the date. You're right—you may not like him very much, or he may not like you. But that's all right. Try to get to know each other. That will only happen if you relax and be yourself. If you're really nervous, you could ask your friend and her boyfriend to join you on a double date. Perhaps you'll feel more relaxed in a group.

Remember, it's only one evening. So have fun. If it doesn't go well, it's no big deal. And maybe you'll be less nervous on your next blind date.
- Ms. Trudy

Brief note
"It's no big deal" means it's not important (so don't worry about it).

B Vocabulary

Write the letters of the words and phrases from the box next to the correct definitions.

a. be yourself	b. get to know (someone)	c. cancel	d. double date	e. hobby
f. be stressed out	g. go on a blind date	h. shy	i. worry	j. perfect

1. to learn about a person and become friendly with each other ______
2. to go out with someone you don't know ______
3. to feel afraid that something bad may happen ______
4. to feel a lot of stress ______
5. something you like to do in your free time; a special interest ______
6. to decide not to go to a planned event ______
7. exactly right; having no bad points ______
8. to relax and not worry what others think ______
9. feeling nervous talking to others ______
10. a date that two couples go on together ______

C In Your World

Make a list of three things you would like to do on a blind date and three things you would not like to do. Then compare your ideas with a partner and discuss your reasons.

Me	
I'd like to	I wouldn't like to
______	______
______	______
______	______

D Grammar

Making predictions and expressing probability with *will* and *be going to*

Brief note

Sentence adverbs usually come at the beginning of a sentence or as part of a phrase at the end.

making predictions			
You can make a prediction (give an opinion about the future) using either *will* or *be going to*. *It'**ll rain** tomorrow.* *It'**s going to** rain tomorrow.*			
expressing probability			
maybe	**possibly**	**perhaps**	**probably**
Maybe is often used as a sentence adverb. It means that something is possible but not certain.	*Possibly* can be used after *will* or *be* verbs and as a sentence adverb. It's not used often in speaking.	*Perhaps* is like *maybe*, but it is used more often in writing than in conversation.	*Probably* is stronger than *maybe*, *possibly*, or *perhaps*. It means you are almost sure.
Maybe they are going to see a movie. I will talk to Jim or **maybe** his sister.	He will **possibly** call us tomorrow. He will call us tomorrow, **possibly**.	**Perhaps** you are going to need more money. We will buy some books and **perhaps** a magazine.	She will **probably** get the job. I am **probably** going to stay home on Sunday.

Brief note

One reason *will possibly* is not often spoken is because *might* or *may* is a more common way to say the same thing.

E Grammar Practice

Fill in the blanks with the words from the box. If more than one answer is possible, select the one that seems best.

possibly	will	is	maybe	probably

1. I think the guests ________________ have a good time.
2. Do you think he ________________ going to call you?
3. ________________ she will enjoy dinner at an Indian restaurant.
4. She's sick, so she's ________________ going to cancel the dinner party.
5. We are ________________ going to get a German car, or perhaps an Italian one. We're not sure.

F Use the Language

Going on a date

Read the following dating situations. What advice do you have for these people? What will probably happen if they take your advice? What if they don't? Make notes about your advice and predictions on a separate piece of paper.

Emma: For our second date, a guy invited me to an art museum. He knows a lot about art, but I don't. What should I do?

Fred: I went on a blind date at my favorite restaurant. She was very interesting, but she was not nice to our waiter. Should I go out with her again?

Pedro: A girl invited me on a bike ride. I really like her—but I can't ride a bike. I'm worried about telling her. Any advice?

Now compare your ideas with a partner's. Report your ideas to the class.

Check Your Progress

1 Fill in the blanks with the correct words from the box.

perfect	stressed	myself	blind	know
double date	hobby	worry	shy	cancel

1. My best friend introduced me to his cousin for a ________________ date.
2. Our date was ________________. It couldn't have been better.
3. I felt ________________ out when I realized I would be late.
4. I hope I can get to ________________ her better the next time we meet.
5. It's hard for me to be ________________ when I want someone to like me.
6. If you need to ________________ the meeting, please call the day before.
7. I'm not very good at meeting new people because I'm ________________.
8. My girlfriend and I have the same ________________. We both like photography.
9. This weekend we have a ________________ with Ben and Dana.
10. Don't ________________. I'm sure your date will go well.

2 Fill in the blanks with *probably*, *possibly*, and *probably not*.

1. It will ____________ be safe to touch this dog.

2. He will ____________ hit the ball.

3. She will ____________ go on a date with him.

4. I couldn't ____________ eat another bite.

3 Fill in the blanks with the correct words from the box.

will	is	perhaps	probably	possibly

On Thursday evening, I ❶ ____________ have a small dinner party. I invited three friends, and I told them to bring one guest. Janet loves spending time with her boyfriend, so she is ❷ ____________ going to bring him. Karen wants to bring her boyfriend too, but he said he ❸ ____________ going to work late that day. ❹ ____________ she will come alone. Stephanie is ❺ ____________ going to bring her friend Mark, but I'm not sure.

5E Going to the Movies

A Model Conversation

Read the conversation. Then listen. Track 062

Chuck: Hi, everyone. Did you choose a movie for tonight?
Bill: I don't know, what do you and Christine think?
Chuck: Well, I think we should see *Victory Parade*.
Christine: Hmm. I'd rather not. It's an action movie, and it might be really violent.
Sarah: If you hate violent action movies, you must hate horror movies, too, right? Because I'd like to see *House of Rats*.
Christine: Sorry, but no—it looks too scary.
Chuck: Well, *Crazy Quentin* ought to be good. It's the number-one movie in online reviews.
Bill: That's an animated movie, right? Based on a fantasy computer game, I believe. That could be fun.
Chuck: I agree. Oh, wait—we can't see it. It's sold out.
Christine: Hey, I know! Let's see *I Truly Do*. It's a romantic comedy. It should be a good movie for a double date, and I heard it's hilarious.

Brief note

If a movie is "sold out", it means no more tickets are available.

B Vocabulary

Match the words with the correct definitions.

1. animated • • **a.** extremely funny
2. violent • • **b.** causing fear
3. scary • • **c.** telling a story through moving pictures drawn by artists
4. hilarious • • **d.** showing people getting hurt

C About You

List two kinds of movies you like and two kinds you don't like. Give one or two examples of each kind. Then tell a partner and give reasons for your opinions.

	Kinds of movies	Examples (titles)
I like	1.	
	2.	
I don't like	1.	
	2.	

D Grammar

Modals of possibility

modals of possibility		
A modal adds meaning to the main verb. Modals of possibility say how sure you are about something.		
meaning	**modals**	**examples**
possibility	*could, may, might*	A: Who's at the door? B: I don't know. It **could** be Jake. Devon **may not** come to the movies with us. I **might** stay home this summer, or I **might** travel. I'm not sure.
strong possibility	*should, ought to*	This movie **ought to** be good. It's very popular. I'm leaving now, so I **should** be home in ten minutes.
certainty	*must, can't*	If you like to laugh, you **must** like comedies. That **can't / must not** be true. It's not possible.

E Grammar Practice

Circle the correct answers.

1. All my friends like this restaurant, so it (could / ought to) have good food.
2. Don't touch that snake! It (can't / should) be safe.
3. Eric is still thinking about his plans for tonight. He (might / can't) visit his parents.
4. Kira's car is here, and her bedroom light is on. She (must / could) be home.
5. I'm really excited to see this movie. It (might / should) be hilarious.
6. Check the date on that meat before you cook it. It (may / must) be old.
7. Tim always wants to see fantasy movies. They (should / must) be his favorite.
8. Maybe we shouldn't watch this movie with the kids. It (could / can't) be violent.

F Use the Language

What does the future hold?

Fifty years in the future, what will the world be like? Talk about the topics below in small groups. What's possible, and what's not? Try to make at least one prediction about each topic. Ask one member of the group to write your predictions down.

Talk about the possible effects of these changes. Will the world be better or worse? Remember to give reasons.

- Food
- Technology
- TV and movies
- Dating, love, and marriage
- Work and jobs
- Education

Now report your group's most interesting predictions to the class.

Check Your Progress

1 **Find and circle the words.**

A	N	I	M	A	T	E	D	O	P	R	O	X	O	G
R	A	O	G	K	D	H	Z	W	V	F	N	Q	F	U
R	O	G	I	F	F	C	L	A	T	Y	G	T	A	O
T	F	M	B	T	O	N	R	M	M	T	T	E	N	U
T	B	M	A	M	C	O	R	U	Z	A	S	W	T	L
Z	A	L	E	N	N	A	L	P	A	C	Y	Q	A	P
O	L	D	A	C	T	J	L	C	C	C	G	Q	S	O
R	Y	D	C	C	S	I	R	O	R	R	O	H	Y	L
I	G	R	G	S	T	Q	C	M	I	N	T	D	L	D

comedy
action
horror
romantic
fantasy
animated

2 **In which kind of movie can you expect the following things?**

1. Car chases and fights: ______________________
2. Something scary that can give you nightmares: ______________________
3. Talking animal characters: ______________________
4. Love stories: ______________________
5. Things that make you laugh: ______________________
6. Things that we can't see in real life: ______________________

3 **Fill in the blanks with the correct words from the box.**

can't should could must

1. The girls ______________ be watching a romantic movie.

2. They're trapped inside during winter. It ______________ be cold there.

3. This movie is romantic, but it ______________ also be a comedy.

4. If it's an action movie, there ______________ probably be some fighting.

4 **Circle the correct answers.**

1. If we don't hurry, we (ought not to / may) be late for the movie.
2. If there are gun fights in the movie, it (may / must) be violent.
3. We (must / should not) go to a movie at midnight if you're tired.

5F Nightlife

A Model Conversation

Brief note

"Feel like" is usually followed by a gerund.
*Do you **feel like** dancing?*

It can also be followed by a noun.
*I **feel like** dessert. = I'd like to eat dessert.*

Read the conversation. Then listen. Track 063

Lawrence: Did you enjoy the concert?
Mary: It was great! I couldn't stop dancing.
Lawrence: Me, neither. Do you feel like dancing more? I know a good club nearby.
Mary: I think I know it, too. Are you talking about Club Blue?
Lawrence: Yes, that's right. It's a fun place.
Mary: Yes, it is. But I'm not sure that I can dance anymore. How about a bar? We can sit down and talk, and maybe have something to eat.
Lawrence: That sounds good. I know one in this neighborhood. My friend is a bartender there, and I'm fairly sure it has no cover charge on weekdays.
Mary: Great!
Lawrence: And it has live music every night. Do you like country music?
Mary: Well… I never listen to it. But I don't mind giving it a try.
Lawrence: Cool. Oh—one more thing. After the band plays, there's karaoke. Can you sing?
Mary: Not at all! I'm really shy in front of big groups!
Lawrence: It's okay. Don't worry. If you don't want to sing, I promise you don't have to.

B Vocabulary

Write the words from the box next to the correct definitions.

dance	bartender	live music	promise	feel like	cover charge	bar	concert

1. ____________________ to want to do (something) right now
2. ____________________ money you have to pay to enter a bar, club, etc.
3. ____________________ to move your body to music
4. ____________________ music played by a singer or band in front of people, not recorded
5. ____________________ a person who makes and sells drinks at a bar
6. ____________________ to say that you will definitely do something
7. ____________________ a business that mostly sells alcoholic drinks
8. ____________________ a live music event, usually held in front of a crowd of people

C In Your World

Think about where you live now or about your hometown. Where can people go to do the following things in the evenings? Which do you like to do? Tell a partner.

Have a romantic date:	Dance:	See a concert:
Eat dinner and hear live music:	Watch or play sports:	Sing karaoke:

D Grammar

that clauses

Brief note

The word *that* is often left out of a *that* clause when speaking informally.

that clauses
Some verbs and adjectives can be followed by a *that* clause. A *that* clause contains a noun and verb. *That* clauses are often used with verbs about thoughts, ideas, speech, and giving advice. *I think **that** swimming is fun. = I think swimming is fun.* *That* clauses can also be used after many adjectives for thoughts, feelings, and possibility. *I'm happy **that** you're here. = I'm happy you're here.*

verbs and adjectives which take *that* clauses					
verbs			**adjectives**		
think	guess	say	certain	aware	likely
believe	know	agree	sure	worried	possible
hope	bet	promise	convinced	hopeful	impossible

Brief note

These verbs include words related to thoughts, ideas, and speech.

Brief note

Adjectives for thoughts, feelings, and possibility are also used with *that*-clauses.

E Grammar Practice

Put the words in order to make sentences.

1. think / you / she / do / come / will ______________________?
2. doctor / I / rest / says / the / should ______________________.
3. you / I / won't / living / here / like / am / worried ______________________.
4. promise / you'll / the / come / party / that / to / me ______________________.
5. I / that / don't / be / care / angry / she'll ______________________.
6. be / it / I'll / late / that / is / possible ______________________.

F Listen to Write

Listen to an advertisement for a new business. What kinds of things can people do there? Put check marks (✓) next to the correct pictures. Track 064

Now, with a partner, plan a business in your town. You want people to come to have fun. What kind of business is it? What can people do there? Write a short advertisement like the one you just heard. Share your advertisement with the class. Whose business sounds like the most fun?

Check Your Progress

1 **Put the conversation in the correct order. Then listen and check your answers.** Track 065

_____ **Iris**: Okay, that could be fun. Where should we go?

_____ **Iris**: You know, I didn't like that bar. Do you have a better idea?

_____ **Ted**: I was certain you'd like my idea, so I bought them last week.

__1__ **Ted**: Let's go out tonight.

_____ **Ted**: Let's go to the bar we went to last week.

_____ **Ted**: Well, if you don't like that, how about going to the theater?

_____ **Iris**: I knew you were planning a surprise! You must have tickets, right?

2 **Write the words from the box next to the correct definitions.**

bartender
cover charge
concert
karaoke
club

1. A person who prepares drinks: ____________________
2. A place to dance: ____________________
3. A music show: ____________________
4. Money that you pay to enter a club or bar: ____________________
5. An activity where customers sing: ____________________

3 **Fill in the blanks with the correct words from the box.**

promise	likely	say	bet	worried

1. It is ____________________ that the theater will be crowded.
2. We ____________________ that our café uses only the best coffee beans from Colombia.
3. Did you ____________________ you never go to bars?
4. He is ____________________ he might not meet someone to dance with.
5. I ____________________ if you ask her on a date, she'll say yes!

4 **Put the words in order to make sentences.**

1. a / she / concert / we / suggests / see

   ____.

2. get / cannot / I / tickets / that / I'm / certain

   ____.

3. restaurant / we / will / food / serve / good / that / the / hope

   ____.

5G Day Trips

A Model Monologues

Brief note

"It's been a long week" means this has been a difficult, stressful week.

Read the conversation. Then listen. Track 066

Dorothy: I'm bored. Let's get out of the house this weekend.

Ned: Are you sure you want to do that? It's been a long week, and I'm stressed out. I suggest we stay in and rest. We could make a plan for next weekend.

Dorothy: But a day trip could relieve your stress. Why not go for a drive somewhere? We could drive up the coast and walk on the beach, go swimming...

Ned: I agree that sounds fun, but did you see the forecast? There might be a big storm.

Dorothy: If the weather's bad, we can go to the music festival downtown. It starts tomorrow.

Ned: But all of those concerts are outdoors!

Dorothy: Oh. Well, if the weather is nice, let's go to the music festival. If it's bad, we should still go to the beach. I promise it'll be relaxing.

Ned: I guess that's a good plan.

B Vocabulary

Listen to the conversation again. Then match the words with the correct definitions.

1. day trip •	• **a.** a special event with many concerts, usually lasting a few days
2. outdoors •	• **b.** the area where the land meets the sea
3. music festival •	• **c.** a trip for only one day
4. relieve •	• **d.** the center of a city or the part with tall buildings, stores, etc.
5. downtown •	• **e.** not inside a building; outside
6. coast •	• **f.** to make (a bad feeling) better

C In Your World

Where can people take day trips in or near your hometown? Think of three places.

1. ______________________

2. ______________________

3. ______________________

Now talk to a partner. Suggest each of these day trips. Give reasons why your suggestions would be fun. Which day trips sound the best?

D Quick Review

Look back at the brief notes in this unit.

1. What does *help yourself* mean?

2. Which sentence sounds more formal: "I think they will arrive soon" or "I think that they are going to arrive soon"?

E Grammar

Suggesting activities

In English, there are several common ways to suggest doing something together.

let's	*suggest (that)*
The most common way to propose something is with *let's* + verb: ***Let's** go!*	Use *suggest* + *that* clause: *I **suggest** that we go to a museum.* *I **suggest** you reserve a table.*
modal verbs, including *shall*	**questions as suggestions**
Could, *should*, and *ought to* are often used for suggestions: *We **could** see a movie.* *We **ought to** visit my parents.* *You **should** book a flight.*	*Why not* + verb: ***Why not** go to the mountains?* *What about* + gerund: ***What about** going to the beach?* *Why don't you* + verb: ***Why don't you** rest this weekend?*

Brief note

Shall is only used in questions, usually with *we*. It is not commonly used.
Shall we get going?

F Grammar Practice

Circle the correct answers.

1. Why not (meet / meeting) at a bar to watch the game?
2. I suggest (go / we go) to a concert this weekend.
3. Let's (plan / planning) a day trip to the coast.
4. It's a beautiful day. We (ought to / suggest) have our lunch outdoors.
5. Dancing might relieve your stress. Why don't you (try / trying) it?
6. I want to visit my grandparents this summer. What about (book / booking) a trip there in July?

G Use the Language

Let's go!

Work in groups of two or three students. Plan a weekend trip together using the suggestions below. Each student should choose a different place. Now suggest that place to your group. Suggest things to do there and give reasons why it is the best choice.

A hotel by the ocean
A beautiful but crowded beach
Swimming and water sports

A house by a lake in the forest
Cheap, quiet, relaxing
No TV and no other people

Downtown in a nearby city
Great nightlife
Expensive

Who gave the best reasons? Where should you go? Try to agree. Then tell the class.

Check Your Progress

1 **Write the words from the box under the correct pictures.**

1. ____________________

2. ____________________

3. ____________________

4. ____________________

coast
festival
downtown
day trip

2 **Match the questions with the correct answers.**

1. What do you think we should do?
2. Shall we take a trip?
3. Do you think we ought to invite Bob and Sally?
4. Couldn't I do the driving?
5. What about renting a car?

- **a.** No, we should go alone this time.
- **b.** Let's not. We can use my brother's.
- **c.** Certainly. I'd like to do that.
- **d.** I suggest we go for a walk on the coast.
- **e.** If you really want to, you may.

3 **Put the words in order to make sentences.**

1. to / you / ought / take / day / trip / a ____________________.
2. let's / at / home / stay / not ____________________.
3. pay / suggests / dinner / for / Frank / he / that ____________________.
4. tickets / shall / plane / I / buy ____________________?
5. at / meet / festival / the / he / us / couldn't ____________________.
6. don't / we / why / cousin / visit / my ____________________?

4 **Listen to four sentences spoken by Marcia. Then circle true or false.** Track 067

1.	Marcia wants to get out of the city for the day.	true	false
2.	She wants to take a long trip.	true	false
3.	She doesn't care too much about spending money.	true	false
4.	She wants to stay near the water.	true	false

Unit Review

A Out on the Town

Read the magazine article about three different districts in one city.

Districts of Berlin

Charlottenburg: If you're interested in fine arts and jazz, then Charlottenburg may be your best choice. Here you can visit the finest museums in the city and a lot of great stores. During the day, you can enjoy a visit to the Berlin zoo. For night owls, there are several exciting jazz clubs to enjoy at night.

Brief note

A *night owl* is a person who is active at night.

Friedrichshain: If you're looking for great nightlife, you might prefer Friedrichshain. There are karaoke clubs, heavy metal clubs, and many bars with some of the best beers in the world.

Kreuzberg and Schöneberg: Here you will find a casual and relaxed area for shopping and eating out. There are parks, a famous outdoor farmer's market, and many international food choices, from Korean to French to local German restaurants.

B Plan Your Day

Work in small groups. You are going to visit Berlin together. Discuss the districts above. Use the Internet to learn more. Which is the most interesting to you? Talk in detail about the things you could do there and the things you would rather not do. Then, as a group, plan your first day in Berlin. Where will you go, and what will you do?

Morning	
Afternoon	
Evening	

C Reminder

Put a check mark (✓) next to the things you can do.

________ Discuss different things to do, places to go, etc.

________ Describe plans, arrangements, and alternatives

________ Understand the main points in short newspaper and magazine articles about current and familiar topics

Further Practice

A Listen for Information

Read and then listen to a speaker talk about her plans for the next year. Take notes about things she will do, things she probably will do, and things she might do. Track 068

Woman: Next year will be a very exciting year for me. I'm graduating from high school, and I'm planning to move out of my parents' house. I'm going to attend a university in Florida. I'll probably live on campus with a roommate. But if I get enough money in loans, it's possible I'll live alone in an apartment. I'm going to study photography. I'd like to have a little photo studio of my own. But that probably won't happen for a year or two.
I should be able to find a part-time job. If I'm lucky, I may get some work doing wedding photography. I'm going to study hard. I'm excited, but I worry that I won't have any time to relax. Do you think I'll be stressed out? I hope not!

will	probably will	might

B Prepare

Now think about a time in your own future. It could be next year, two years from now, or any other time you choose. Write some notes below about what you will do, what you probably will do, and what you might do but aren't sure about yet.

C Speak

Using the notes you have prepared, tell a group of your classmates about your future plans. After you've presented some ideas, invite your classmates to ask you questions.

MEMO

UNIT 6 Staying Fit

Scan and find the tracks.

Before You Read

◆ **Talk about these questions with your classmates.**

1. Why do some people live longer than others?
2. What are some things that you can do to live longer?
3. Who is the oldest person in your family? How old is he or she?

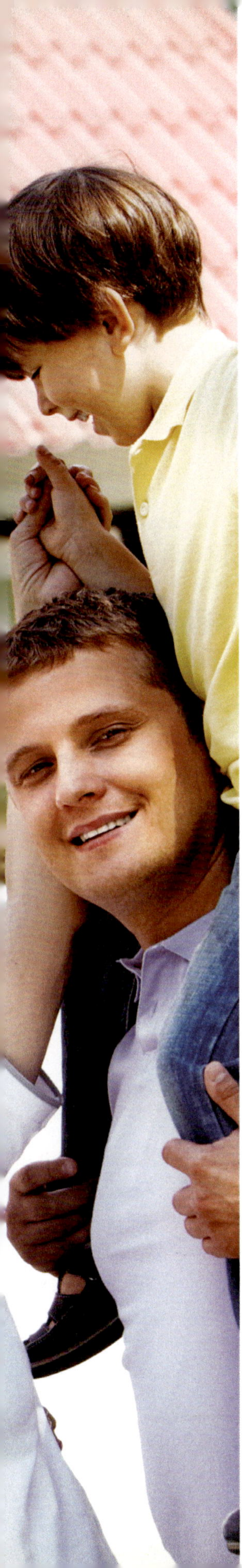

Vocabulary

◆ **Read the definitions. Then match each word in bold with its definition.**

A. one of the things that cause something to happen
B. the amount of time something lasts
C. passed down from older family members to younger ones at birth
D. to remain strong against something
E. drinks such as beer and wine
F. to help cause a result
G. a set of signs that passes information from one person to another
H. the chance of something bad happening

1. ______ Diseases and resistance to them can be **genetic**.

2. ______ A balanced diet **contributes** to a long and healthy life.

3. ______ A diet that is low in fat and sugar lessens the **risk** of some diseases.

4. ______ What our parents pass down to us at birth can either increase or decrease the **length** of our lives.

5. ______ Drinking too much **alcohol** is unhealthy.

6. ______ Scientists have found that many **factors** contribute to a long and healthy life.

7. ______ Our genetic **codes** play a part in how long we live.

8. ______ Some people naturally **resist** diseases that could kill them.

Living Right to Live Long

Track 069

We all want to live long lives. Some things we have control over and others we do not. Certain choices affect our health. Knowing what is healthy for our bodies is the key to living a long life.

Our genetic codes play a part in how long we live. They can either increase or decrease the length of our lives. Some people naturally resist diseases that could kill them, while others are more likely to have problems such as cancer or heart disease.

Recent studies, however, have shown that how we live our lives might be more important than genetics. Most things about our health are within our control. Scientists

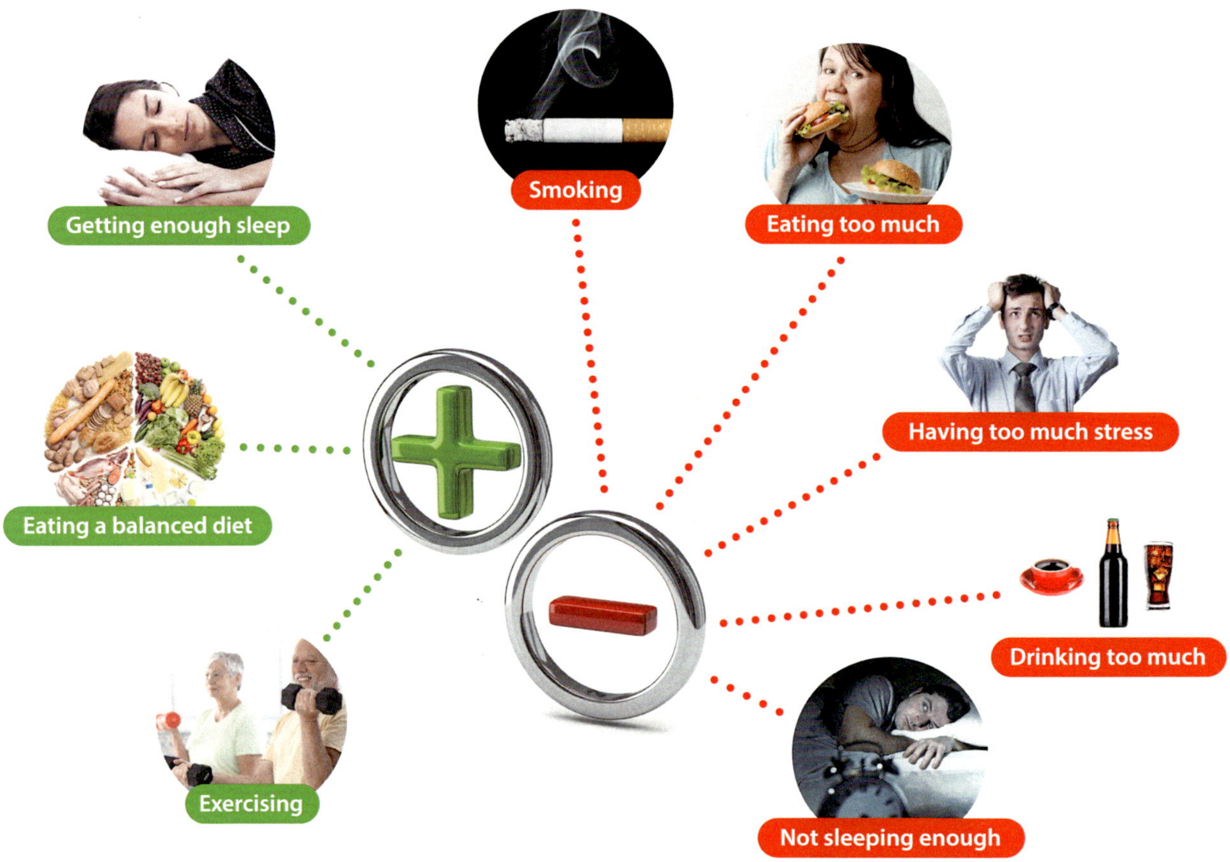

▲ Positive and negative influences on longevity

have found that many factors contribute to long and healthy lives. For instance, eating a balanced diet of foods which are low in fat and sugar lessens the risk of heart disease and cancer. Exercising can also reduce body fat and strengthen our hearts. In addition, exercising helps us to feel better physically and mentally. Positive daily choices make a difference in how long we live.

Simply not doing certain negative things can also greatly improve our health. Smoking, eating too much food, and drinking too much alcohol, coffee, and soft drinks are all unhealthy. Stress and lack of sleep are also bad for us. Once in a while, these things will not hurt us, but they can when done too often.

The choices that we make from day to day are important. They can either add or subtract years from our lives. Living longer is a choice!

Review the Highlights

◆ **Mark up the text and infographic according to the instructions.**

1. Look at Paragraph 1. Underline the information about control and choices.
2. Look at Paragraph 2. Put stars next to what our genetic codes can do to the lengths of our lives.
3. Look at Paragraph 3. Underline how we can lessen our risk for getting cancer and heart disease.
4. Look at Paragraph 4. Put a star next to how often we can do certain negative things without hurting ourselves.
5. Look at the infographic. Circle the information in the reading that goes with each picture in the infographic.

Check Your Comprehension

◆ **Circle the correct answer.**

1. What is the message of the passage? Main idea
   a. People have complete control over how long they live.
   b. People have absolutely no control over how long they live.
   c. People have no control over what and how much they eat.
   d. People have more control than they think over how long they live.

2. What is the one thing that we cannot control? Details: what
   a. What we eat
   b. Where we live and work
   c. Our genetic code
   d. Our exercise plans

3. Based on the reading, what can be inferred about cancer? Inference
   a. Cancer is a disease that only attacks the heart.
   b. Cancer is not caused by genetics.
   c. Eating unhealthy foods can increase your risk for getting cancer.
   d. Cancer is only caused by genetics.

4. How often can we make negative health choices without hurting ourselves? Fact
   a. Once in a while
   b. Always
   c. Usually
   d. Never

5. Which is NOT a choice that will subtract years from your life? Negative fact
   a. Going jogging three times a week
   b. Sleeping an average of 5.5 hours per night
   c. Drinking soft drinks
   d. Working a stressful job

◆ **Complete the summary. Write the words from the reading that best fit in the blanks. One word is extra.**

length factors resisting risk contribute codes alcohol genetic

We cannot control exactly how long we live, but there are some choices that we can make in order to live longer. Recent studies have shown that how we live our lives might be more important than our 1. ______________ 2. ______________. On the one hand, eating a healthy, balanced diet and exercising are both 3. ______________ that 4. ______________ to longevity. On the other hand, smoking, eating too much food, and drinking unhealthy drinks such as 5. ______________, coffee, or soft drinks are all things that subtract years from our lives. Too much stress and too little sleep are also things that take away from the 6. ______________ of our lives. 7. ______________ bad choices and making healthy choices for our bodies is an important part of living a long life.

Linked Skills Activity

◆ **Read the passage below with a partner. Then work with your partner to make a list of jobs that people do in order to help others live longer and happier lives.**

There are a lot of people in this world who make careers out of helping us live longer and happier lives. Some people teach us how to eat or cook more healthily, or even come to our houses and cook healthy meals for us. Other people plan our exercise routines. Some people help us relax or teach us how to cut the stress out of our lives. And yet others help us resist our desires to drink alcohol, eat too much food, or smoke cigarettes.

Jobs That Help Other People Live Longer Lives

counselors, nurses...

◆ **Interview your partner about the healthy and unhealthy life choices that he or she made this week. Use the questions below as a guide.**

What do you do that makes you happy?
What are some things that might make you live longer?
What healthy and unhealthy foods have you eaten this week?
How well did you sleep this week?
How many times did you exercise this week?
How many soft drinks did you have this week?
Did you smoke or drink alcohol this week?
Were you stressed out last week?

◆ **Write a paragraph about your partner's life. Based on the answers given, is your partner adding or subtracting time to his or her life? Share your paragraph with the rest of your classmates.**

____

____

____

Taekwondo at Keimyung University

Track 070

[**KMU Core Competency:** Adaptability]

Taekwondo is one of the most respected programs at Keimyung University, blending tradition with modern education. The Taekwondo Department offers a well-rounded curriculum that combines theoretical learning with hands-on practice, helping students master this martial art while developing valuable life skills. Through their studies, students gain practical expertise, leadership qualities, and a solid understanding of sports science. These courses also encourage critical thinking and problem-solving, preparing students for competitions, careers, and personal growth.

Every year, the department hosts dynamic events, including Poomsae and sparring competitions, as well as the Keimyung Hanmaul Taekwondo Festival. These activities give students opportunities to test their skills, build confidence, and face new challenges. By participating, students not only improve their physical fitness but also strengthen their mental focus and determination—traits that are essential in Taekwondo and in life.

The department also provides exciting opportunities for international experience. During summer and winter breaks, students can train in countries such as the United States, Canada, and various European nations. These programs broaden their global perspective and demonstrate how Taekwondo unites people across cultures. Closer to home, students take part in Taekwondo exhibitions and national team selection trials, gaining practical experience and professional exposure in real-world settings.

Taekwondo at Keimyung University is more than just a sport. It symbolizes discipline, cultural heritage, and **adaptability**, shaping students into capable individuals ready to meet challenges both inside and outside the *dojang*.

Check Your Comprehension

1. What do students learn in the Taekwondo major?
   (A) Leadership skills
   (B) How to apply sports science
   (C) Expertise through knowledge and practice
   (D) All of the above

2. Where can Taekwondo students gain more experience in Taekwondo?
   (A) The United States
   (B) Japan
   (C) Russia
   (D) China

3. What is the annual event hosted by the KMU Taekwondo Department?
   (A) World Martial Arts Festival
   (B) Hanmaeum Taekwondo Festival
   (C) Hanmaul Taekwondo Festival
   (D) World Taekwondo Culture Festival

Talk or Write about It

1. Why are sports important? What benefits do they bring to people?

   ____

   ____

2. What lessons or skills can you learn by playing a sport?

   ____

   ____

3. Do you think it is better to play sports competitively or just for fun? Why?

   ____

   ____

6C Watching Sports on TV

A Model Conversation

Read the conversation. Then listen. Track 071

Oscar: Look, the Olympics are on.

Karen: Oh, good. What events?

Oscar: Right now, it's surfing and diving.

Karen: I don't really like those. When will gymnastics be on?

Oscar: Not today. So, you like watching gymnastics?

Karen: Yeah, it's my favorite summer event. The athletes are able to do such difficult moves and still look graceful.

Oscar: They are pretty amazing.

Karen: As a kid, I dreamed about competing in an Olympic gymnastics event.

Oscar: Really? I wanted to be an Olympic athlete, too, but in skiing. Sadly, I never go skiing these days. And I wasn't good at it, anyway.

Karen: I'm terrible at gymnastics. So I guess we'll never be great athletes.

Oscar: No. But it's still fun to watch them on TV.

Brief note

"The Olympics" = the Olympic Games. An "event" is a specific race, game, or other competition in the Olympics.

B Vocabulary

Listen to the words. Then match each word with the correct definition. Track 072

1. move •	• **a.** a person who does a sport
2. compete •	• **b.** able to move in a beautiful way
3. terrible •	• **c.** to think about something you really want to do or be
4. athlete •	• **d.** extremely bad
5. graceful •	• **e.** to enter a game or contest and try to win
6. dream •	• **f.** an action of the body

C About You

As a kid, did you dream of being an athlete? If yes, in what sport? If not, what did you dream of being? Think about your answers to the questions. Then share them with a partner.

D Grammar

Gerunds and infinitives

Brief note

The phrase *be able to* means *can*. But it can be used after a modal verb. You cannot use *can* after another modal verb.
(✓) *She might be able to compete in the Olympics.*
(X) *She might ~~can~~ compete in the Olympics.*

gerunds (verb-*ing*)	infinitives (*to* + verb)
As the subject of a sentence or after the *be* verb: ***Swimming*** *is my favorite sport.* *My favorite sport is* ***swimming****.*	After certain verbs (for example, *like, choose, agree, want*): *We* ***agreed to meet*** *on Sunday.* ***Try to eat*** *more vegetables.*
After a preposition: *He is good* ***at writing*** *in English.* *I'm interested* ***in skiing****.*	After some adjectives (for example, *fun, able, nice*): *The X Games are* ***fun to watch****.* *The athletes are* ***able to do*** *graceful moves.*
After certain verbs (for example, *like, enjoy, mind, practice*): *I* ***enjoy watching*** *the Olympics.* *Would you* ***mind closing*** *the window?*	After *know how*: *I* ***know how to swim*** *well.* *Do you* ***know how to play*** *the guitar?*
After *go* (for example, *shopping, dancing,* and some other activities): *Let's* ***go shopping/surfing****.* *We're* ***going swimming/running****.*	

Brief note

Some verbs can be followed by either a gerund or an infinitive. They include *like, love, hate, start,* and *begin*.

E Grammar Practice

Circle the correct answers. If both answers are possible, circle both.

1. I have to practice (to sing / singing) this song.
2. Are you good at (to get / getting) to know new people?
3. Patrick wasn't able (to find / finding) a seat.
4. Does the teacher want (to talk / talking) to me?
5. You don't have to walk to school. I don't mind (to drive / driving) you.
6. Do you know how (to cook / cooking)?
7. We usually go (to run / running) in the morning.
8. My sister loves (to go / going) surfing in the summer.
9. That actor is fun (to watch / watching) on the screen.
10. The class started (to laugh / laughing).

F Use the Language

Watching sports

Talk with one or two partners about their favorite athlete, their favorite sport to watch, and the reasons for their choices. Take notes and fill in the chart.

Name		
Favorite athlete		
Reason(s)		
Favorite sport to watch		
Reason(s)		

Share your chart with the class. Who gave the most surprising answers? The most interesting reasons?

Check Your Progress

1 **Listen to the conversation. Then choose the correct answers.** Track 073

Tony: Did you see any of the Olympics on TV this past week?

Sarah: Yeah, I sure did! I like watching the figure skating—the skaters are so graceful! I think skiing is on later today.

Tony: Skiing? Cool! When I was a kid, I was able to ski pretty well.

Sarah: Really? I tried it once, and I was pretty terrible at it. But I loved skating with my friends. I know how to do a few moves.

Tony: You have to show me sometime. I didn't know you were an athlete.

Sarah: I'm not, really… but you are! Don't you have diving practice today?

Tony: Actually, in ten minutes! I'd better run. Let's go swimming together sometime. Bye!

Sarah: Bye!

1.	Sarah	a. watched the Olympics.	b. was good at skiing.	c. was good at diving.
2.	Tony	a. can ski well now.	b. is skiing later today.	c. was able to ski well.
3.	Sarah was	a. not good at skiing.	b. really good at skiing.	c. better at diving.
4.	Tony asks Sarah	a. to show him some moves.	b. to watch the Olympics.	c. to meet in ten minutes.
5.	Sarah knows	a. who teaches diving.	b. how to do a few moves.	c. where Tony goes diving.

2 **Listen again and complete the sentences with words from the conversation.**

1. Every four years, you can watch the biggest sporting event in the world, called the ______________.
2. I love swimming, but I enjoy ______________ the most. I love to jump into the water!
3. I'm learning some new ______________ in my gymnastics class. Watch this!
4. Another name for ice dancing is ______________.
5. I am ______________ at skiing—I always fall down.
6. My brother is a great ______________. He plays a lot of sports at his high school.

3 **Fill in the blanks with the correct forms of the verbs.**

1. My sister really enjoys ______________ (dance) to country music.
2. The X Games are so exciting ______________ (watch).
3. Jessica is good at ______________ (play) hockey.
4. Would you mind ______________ (help) me with this equipment?
5. I agreed ______________ (attend) my friend's figure skating event.

4 **Look at the picture and write sentences that describe it. Use a gerund or infinitive in each sentence.**

6D We'd Better Show up Early

A Model Conversation

Read the conversation. Then listen. Track 074

Hailey: Hey, Ben. You weren't in class yesterday—were you sick?

Ben: No, I'm fine. I went to cheer for my brother Ethan's college basketball team. It was such an excellent game.

Hailey: Oh, yeah? What happened?

Ben: They were behind by one point, and there were five seconds left. Then Ethan got the ball and scored. It was incredible.

Hailey: Wow! So, I guess your brother's a good player?

Ben: The best on the team—and it's a good team. I highly recommend you go and watch sometime. In fact, I'm going to their game on Wednesday, if you're free.

Hailey: I am. What time?

Ben: It starts at 7:00 p.m., but we'd better show up early to get good seats. Can you meet me here at 6:15?

Brief note

Use the preposition "on" to talk about being part of a team.
*My friend Claire is **on** that team.*

B Vocabulary

Write the words from the box next to the correct definitions.

basketball	excellent	show up	left	score	second	behind

1. ______________ to get a point or points in a game
2. ______________ 1/60 of a minute
3. ______________ to arrive at a place
4. ______________ having fewer points than the other person or team in a game
5. ______________ extremely good; fantastic
6. ______________ a sport in which players score by throwing a ball through a net (basket)
7. ______________ not used or finished yet; remaining

Match the parts to make sentences.

8. I waited for her for an hour, but she didn't •
9. Oh, we missed the game. There's only •
10. They're not going to win. They're behind •
11. If you're very tall, people might think you're •
12. I suggest you ask Rita to be on your team. She's •
13. Our basketball team played well. We scored •

• **a.** by twenty-two points.
• **b.** an excellent athlete.
• **c.** ninety points.
• **d.** one minute left.
• **f.** show up.
• **g.** good at basketball.

C About You

Are you punctual? Do you arrive early to events or are you always late? Talk to a partner about your time management skills.

D Grammar

Suggestions and advice with gerunds, infinitives, modals, and *that* clauses

suggestions and advice with gerunds and infinitives	
I suggest / I recommend + gerund	
*I **recommend watching** the basketball game on TV.*	*I **suggest going** on the weekend.*
Using *I suggest/recommend* + gerund sounds more formal than using infinitives or modal verbs.	
be sure / it's a good idea + infinitive	
Be sure to go to a game.	**It's a good idea to get** tickets early.
strong advice with the modal *had better*	**suggestions with *that* clauses**
subject + (*had*) *better* + verb	*I suggest/recommend* + *that* clause
We**'d better show up** early to get good seats. = We **better show up** early to get good seats.	I **recommend (that)** she go and watch the game. = I **suggest (that)** she go and watch the game.

Brief note

Informally, people often leave out *had*.

Brief note

In the *that* clause, use the base form of the verb with all subjects:
(✓) *I suggest (that) she/he/it go...*
(X) *I suggest (that) she/he/it goes...*

E Grammar Practice

Fill in the blanks with the correct words from the box.

better idea sure suggest bring inviting that

1. I ______________ that you stay. There are only ten minutes left in the game.
2. Be ______________ to see the college volleyball team sometime!
3. You'd better ______________ a warm coat. It's going to be cold later.
4. I recommended ______________ lots of friends to the game.
5. It's a good ______________ to watch the game on TV.
6. I recommend ______________ we sit near the front.
7. Jim's team had ______________ practice more. They never win any games.

F Use the Language

Let's catch a game!

Go online and research a sporting event that will happen soon in your area. Then suggest to a partner that you both attend and explain why it would be fun. Discuss what you need to do to go to the event. Share your plans with the class.

Check Your Progress

1 Find and circle the words.

S	X	B	L	A	R	X	J	P	V	R	L	K	V	F
T	P	U	U	Z	K	W	G	L	E	U	Y	B	S	D
S	L	N	X	L	L	A	B	T	E	K	S	A	B	N
J	X	D	Y	I	C	W	K	M	G	G	B	A	A	T
F	B	E	H	I	N	D	B	Y	N	O	L	S	F	K
B	D	C	R	S	I	W	G	S	C	O	R	E	N	N
G	E	T	N	E	L	L	E	C	X	E	L	O	R	G
K	K	V	U	C	C	Z	S	H	O	W	U	P	R	E
Q	D	S	P	O	U	E	I	Z	J	G	F	F	Z	O
G	D	N	A	N	I	G	O	U	K	W	C	K	Z	U
Q	C	X	V	D	A	M	J	N	U	H	X	B	D	S
U	D	O	B	U	X	H	O	X	K	D	B	O	I	H
R	B	R	C	R	C	B	L	V	Z	P	J	Q	L	K
L	J	A	O	V	E	M	Z	R	R	S	N	Q	F	Y
U	Q	H	Y	H	J	Y	H	Y	J	H	U	T	I	O

basketball
excellent
show up
left
score
second
behind by

2 Read the monologue. Underline all the suggestions.

So, my friend invited me to see her college field hockey game. Her team is the best in the city. She recommended showing up early to get good seats. She also suggested that I bring some friends. My brother said it was a good idea to bring something to drink because it can get hot sitting in the sun. The game was excellent! The crowd was noisy and excited. We had a lot of fun. My friend was the star of the team. She scored 10 points! Next time, my friends and I had better bring some more comfortable chairs—we sat on the grass for two hours!

3 Read each person's comment. Then write one or two suggestions for each.

My family needs to spend more time together.

____

____

I can't concentrate on my schoolwork.

____

____

My friend and I had an argument.

____

____

6E I Want to Get in Shape

A Model Conversation

Read the conversation. Then listen. Track 075

Brief note

"Work out" is a verb. *Workout* is a noun.
*Did you **work out** today?*
*How was your **workout**?*

Sophia: Excuse me. I just worked out here for the first time, and I'm interested in joining the gym.
Marc: Excellent. Let's talk about your options. You can buy a two-month, six-month, or one-year membership.
Sophia: Hmm. I'll take the two-month membership. I'll be studying in the fall. I probably won't be working out often.
Marc: Okay. And what are your fitness goals?
Sophia: I don't want to lose weight. I just want to get in shape. I'd like to be stronger and have more energy.
Marc: Those are good goals. I recommend that you lift weights and join a yoga class. Yoga classes are included with your membership.
Sophia: Maybe I will try it. Are there any classes today?
Marc: No, but I'll be teaching yoga all afternoon tomorrow, from 1:00 to 5:00. Try to stop by then.

B Vocabulary

Read the words. Then listen to the definitions. Write the letters of the definitions next to the correct words. Then look up the definitions in the dictionary. Track 076

1. work out ________ **2.** lose weight ________ **3.** join ________ **4.** get in shape ________

Fill in the blanks with the correct words from the box.

energy	fitness	strong	membership	lift weights

5. I recommend getting a three-month ____________________ to a gym if you want to get in shape.
6. I don't have much ____________________ in the morning. I usually feel tired.
7. Let's ask Gary to move the sofa. He's really ____________________.
8. If you ____________________ every week, you will get stronger.
9. Mika works at a gym, so she knows a lot about ____________________.

C Comprehension

Listen to the model conversation again. Then answer the questions with complete sentences.

1. What did Sophia do for the first time? A: She ____________________.
2. What membership will Sophia get? A: She will ____________________.
3. What will she be doing in the fall? A: She will be ____________________.
4. What are her fitness goals? A: She wants ____________________, ____________________, ____________________.
5. What does Marc recommend? A: He recommends that ____________________.
6. What will Marc be doing tomorrow afternoon? A: He'll be ____________________.

D Grammar

Future continuous tense

future continuous tense	
You can use the future continuous to talk about future actions that continue for a period of time. It is formed with *will / be going to* + *be* + verb-*ing*.	
a future action lasting for a while	
with *will*	with *be going to*
We**'ll be studying** in Canada for three months. She **won't be working** Friday evening. **Will** you **be working** on weekdays?	I**'m going to be teaching** yoga this afternoon. They**'re not going to be practicing** next weekend. **Are** you **going to be studying** for the test tonight?
a future action happening at a specific time	
Meet me after class. I**'ll be waiting** outside.	They **aren't going to be working** on Sunday.

E Grammar Practice

Circle the correct answers.

1. I'll (be working / working) out tomorrow at 5:00 a.m.
2. You're going (be / to be) waiting in line for a long time.
3. When you come home, I'll (going to be / be) making dinner.
4. We aren't (going to / will) be sitting in class all day.
5. (Will / Are) you going to be staying with relatives during the break?
6. Will (they be / they) studying all night?

F Use the Language

What will you be doing?

You want to get in shape, so you'll be working out and playing sports a lot on weekends. Fill in the chart with different kinds of exercise or sports. Note the time when you will be doing each. (Leave some free time!)

	Fitness Schedule		
	Morning	Afternoon	Evening
Saturday	Time: From to	Time: From to	Time: From to
Sunday	Time: From to	Time: From to	Time: From to

Work with a partner. You want to hang out with him or her this weekend. Ask each other questions about what you will be doing this weekend at different times. Try to find a time when you are both free to meet. Find out if you will be doing any of the same exercises or sports. Suggest doing something together.

Check Your Progress

1 **Read the email. Circle the correct answers. Then listen and check your answers.** Track 077

> Hey, Mike.
>
> I (1) (started / will be starting) at my new gym today. The workout was really hard! My personal trainer, Joe, was really helpful. He (2) (trains / will be training) me for the next few weeks. (3) (I'm going to be hiking / I'll hike) through the Amazon rainforest for a few months next summer, and I want to get in shape for that. I think it's going to take a long time for me to get strong enough! (4) (I trying / I'll try) my best, though.
>
> How are you? (5) (Do you visit / Will you be visiting) sometime soon? I would love to show you around campus. Maybe (6) (I'll be taking / I'll take) you to the gym, too! How's your new yoga class? My sister (7) (will teach / is going to be teaching) at a yoga school next month.
>
> Hope to hear from you soon,
>
> Beth

2 **Listen to the email again. Then answer the questions.**

1. Where is Beth planning to go next summer? ______________________
2. Why does she want to get in shape? ______________________
3. What is Beth's sister doing next month? ______________________
4. What does Mike do for exercise? ______________________

3 **What will you be doing next summer? Think about your plans and write three sentences describing what you will be doing. Then share your answers with a partner. Discuss your plans.**

____

____

____

4 **Unscramble each word or phrase. Then write a sentence using each one.**

1. nergye ____________ ______________________
2. sfstnei ____________ ______________________
3. grnsto ____________ ______________________
4. smbhpeerim ____________ ______________________
5. fitl ghwiets ____________ ______________________
6. rowk tou ____________ ______________________
7. osel withge ____________ ______________________
8. oinj ____________ ______________________
9. teg ni hspea ____________ ______________________

6F Fitness Tips

A Authentic Text: Workout guide

Read the text. Then listen. Track 078

Brief note

The phrase "get your money's worth" means to get a good deal. It means you are happy and don't feel that you paid too much money.

Are you a new gym member? Do you want to get your money's worth? Follow our advice.

1. Nutrition is very important. Have a healthy snack an hour before your workout. Fruit, for example, will give you lots of energy. After your workout, it is recommended that you have a meal with lots of protein. Protein helps your muscles grow. Eggs, cheese, and chicken are good choices.
2. It's very important that you learn to use the treadmill and other pieces of exercise equipment correctly. If you don't, you might get hurt. Ask an employee for help.
3. Personal trainers are expensive. But if you are a new member, many gyms offer a free lesson with a trainer. Try it! You will learn a lot. It's not necessary that you pay for more lessons.

Brief note

A "treadmill" is a machine for walking and running.

B Vocabulary

Match the words with the correct definitions.

1. necessary
2. healthy
3. free
4. important
5. nutrition

- **a.** needed
- **b.** the process of eating the right kinds of food to be healthy
- **c.** available without paying money; at no cost
- **d.** good for your body
- **e.** having a lot of value; serious

C About You

Do you worry about your nutrition? What are your eating habits? Share with a partner. Discuss who eats healthier and why.

D Grammar

Empty *it* and *that* clauses

Brief note

The subject in these sentences is called "empty *it*" because *it* does not stand for a noun. Other kinds of sentences with empty *it* include:
*A: What time is **it**?* *B: **It**'s 3:30.*
*A: How far is **it** to the gym?* *B: **It**'s two kilometers.*

It is + adjective + ***that*** clause	
It is + adjective + *that* clause can be used with certain adjectives to talk about suggestions, rules, and recommendations. These adjectives include *recommended, important, necessary,* and *required*.	
Having a meal with protein is recommended.	= ***It is recommended that*** *you have a meal with protein.*
Learning to use the exercise equipment is important.	= ***It's important that*** *you learn to use the exercise equipment.*
Paying for more lessons is not necessary (for you).	= ***It's not necessary that*** *you pay for more lessons.*
Paying for more lessons is not required (for her).	= ***It is not required that*** *she pay for more lessons.*
You can also use *it is* + adjective + *that* clause with some other adjectives about opinions. These adjectives include *good, great, amazing, terrible,* and *possible*.	
It's possible that I'll join a gym.	**It's great that** he's eating healthy foods.

Brief note

In *that* clauses about suggestions, rules, etc., use the base form of the verb with all subjects. In these sentences, you cannot leave out *that*.
(✓) *It's important that* ***he/she learn*** *to use the exercise equipment.*
(X) *It's important he/she learns to use the exercise equipment.*

E Grammar Practice

Rewrite the sentences using *It's* and a *that* clause.

1. Drinking water on a hot day is important. ____________________

2. Talking to your doctor is necessary. ____________________

3. Taking long walks is recommended. ____________________

4. He never eats vegetables. That's terrible. ____________________

F Use the Language

Health and fitness questionnaire

Complete the following questionnaire about your health and fitness. Then ask a partner the questions and write his or her answers in short sentences. Do you have similar answers? How are your answers different?

Me	My Partner (Name: ____________________)
1. What kind of exercise do you like?	**1.** What kind of exercise do you like?
2. How good is your health? (Circle one.) Excellent Good Average Bad	**2.** How good is your health? (Circle one.) Excellent Good Average Bad
3. How often do you eat healthy meals? Always Usually Sometimes Never	**3.** How often do you eat healthy meals? Always Usually Sometimes Never
4. What are some healthy foods?	**4.** What are some healthy foods?
5. How could you improve your health?	**5.** How could you improve your health?

Share some recommendations about how to live a healthier life with your partner. Do you think these are good recommendations? Share your ideas with the class.

Check Your Progress

1 Complete the crossword.

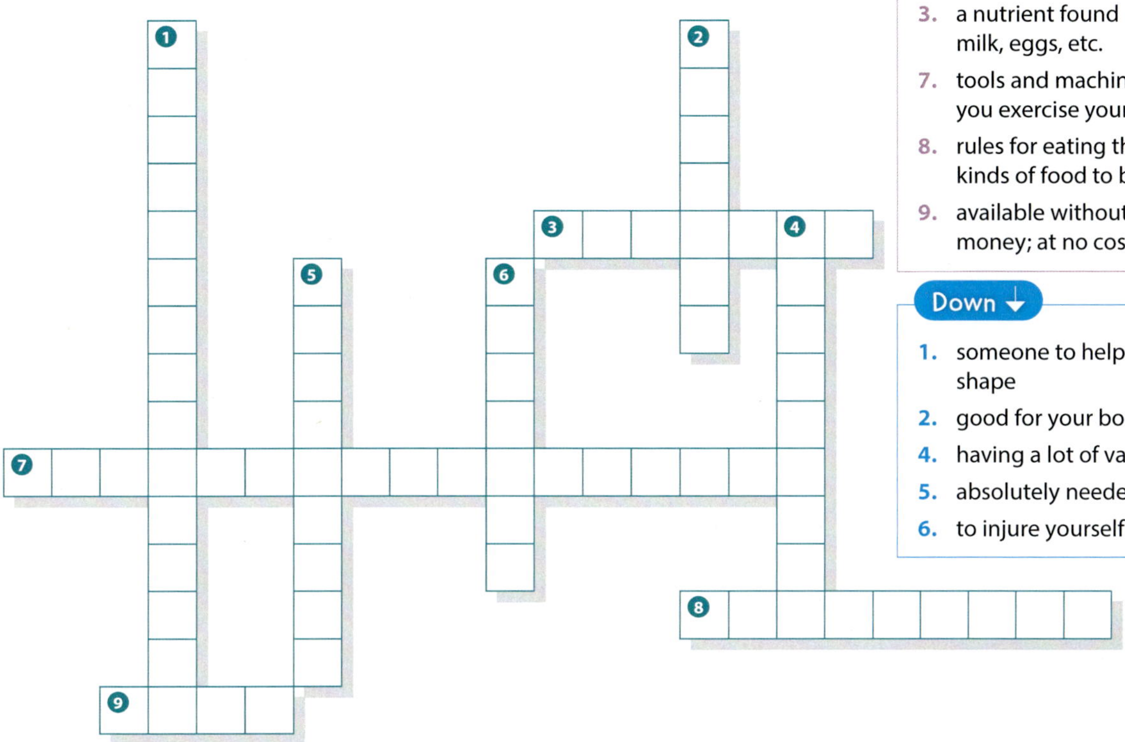

Across →

3. a nutrient found in meat, milk, eggs, etc.
7. tools and machines to help you exercise your muscles
8. rules for eating the right kinds of food to be healthy
9. available without paying money; at no cost

Down ↓

1. someone to help you get in shape
2. good for your body
4. having a lot of value; serious
5. absolutely needed
6. to injure yourself

2 Listen to Sandy and circle true or false. Track 079

1.	Sandy is talking about her personal trainer.	true	false
2.	Tony says that eating breakfast every day is important.	true	false
3.	Sandy has to pay for nutrition classes at the gym.	true	false
4.	Tony says that it's important that Sandy learn how to use the equipment.	true	false
5.	Sandy doesn't like her new healthy lifestyle.	true	false

3 Put the words in order to make sentences.

1. it / exercise / is / important / eat / that / after / you / well / you

____.

2. it / not / is / required / that / bring / you / your / weights / own / to / the / gym

____.

3. it / is / that / necessary / you / entering / shower / pool / before / the

____.

4. several / it's / great / you're / that / week / working / out / times / a

____.

6G At the Doctor's Office

A Model Monologues

Read the conversation. Then listen. Track 080

Brief note

"I can't keep anything down" means you keep vomiting whenever you eat anything.

Doctor: Hi, Robin. What seems to be the problem?
Patient: Well, doctor, I've had nausea for the last two days. I can't keep anything down.
Doctor: Have you had any other symptoms? Headache? Fever? Body aches? Anything like that?
Patient: Yes, I had a stomachache and body aches yesterday. They're gone now. I feel a little better, but I still can't eat.
Doctor: Hmm. Have you eaten any bad-tasting food recently—especially chicken, eggs, or seafood?
Patient: I don't think so. I had lunch the other day at a seafood restaurant, but the food tasted fine.
Doctor: Well, it sounds like food poisoning to me, but it's hard to know for sure. You're already getting better, so my advice is to rest and drink lots of water or juice.
Patient: You can't give me a prescription?
Doctor: Sorry, the only cure for food poisoning is time. You can buy pills for the nausea at any pharmacy, but it might not help. If your nausea isn't gone in a few days, then call me again.

B Vocabulary: Symptoms

Listen to the list of symptoms. Then write the letter of the correct definition next to each. Track 081

1. nausea ____
2. sore throat ____
3. body aches ____
4. cough ____
5. runny nose ____
6. fever ____
7. congestion ____
8. allergy ____

a. a high body temperature
b. a feeling of sickness; wanting to vomit
c. having liquid come from your nose
d. pain all over the body
e. a painful feeling in your throat (inside your neck)
f. a blocked nose; trouble breathing through your nose
g. getting ill from a specific thing (a food, an animal, a medication, etc.)
h. to push air out suddenly from your throat with a noise

C Vocabulary in Context

Listen to the words and their definitions. Practice saying the words out loud. Then fill in the blanks with the correct words. Track 082

cure: a way to stop a medical problem
food poisoning: illness from eating spoiled (not fresh) or incorrectly cooked food
gone: no longer there; (of a symptom) having stopped
pill: a small, circle-shaped piece of medication
prescription: a note from a doctor to a pharmacist about medication for a patient

1. Take one ________________ three times a day with meals.
2. The doctor gave me a ________________ for some headache medication. Now my pain is ________________!
3. There is no ________________ for a cold, but medicine can help with the symptoms.
4. Always be sure to cook chicken well, or you might get ________________.

D Grammar

Present perfect vs. simple past

present perfect vs. simple past		
present perfect	Use the present perfect to talk about an action or state that is not finished. It has a connection to the present.	
	I**'ve lived** here for three years. (I moved here three years ago, and I still live here.)	
	Use the present perfect when the time of a past action is not important or not known.	
	I **haven't had** the flu for a long time.	We**'ve** already **seen** that movie.
simple past	Use the simple past to talk about an action or state that happened in the past and is finished.	
	I **lived** there for three years. (I do not live there anymore. I have moved.)	
	Use the simple past with past time expressions.	
	I **had** the flu **last week**, but I'm better now.	We **saw** that movie **yesterday**.

E Grammar Practice

Fill in the blanks with the correct forms of the verbs in parentheses.

1. My dad ________________ (feel) terrible last night.
2. You ________________ (forget) to take your pills this morning.
3. ________________ you ever ________________ (see) this doctor before?
4. I'm very healthy. I ________________ (not get) sick for years!
5. She ________________ (have) an allergy to cats since she was about 4 years old.
6. I ________________ (take) that medicine for a week and then stopped.
7. He ________________ (have) a severe cough yesterday, but it's gone now.
8. Maria ________________ already ________________ (tell) the doctor about her sore throat and body aches.

F Use the Language

I have never told a lie!

Write ten sentences about yourself. Some sentences should be true, and others should be lies. Write about things in the past, or things that started in the past and continue until now.

Then get in small groups. Share your sentences with the group. Your group will guess if your sentence is true or a lie. Each correct guess gets one point. The person with the most points at the end is the winner.

Ten things about me	
1.	**6.**
2.	**7.**
3.	**8.**
4.	**9.**
5.	**10.**

Check Your Progress

1 **Write the words from the box under the correct pictures.**

nausea	fever	stomachache	sore throat	cough	runny nose	prescription	pills

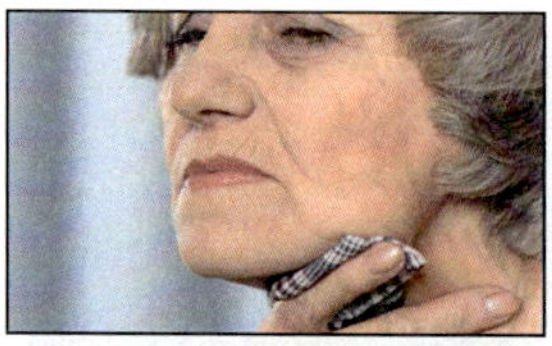

1. ____________

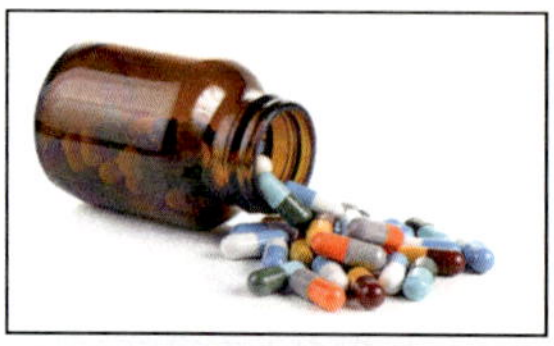

2. ____________

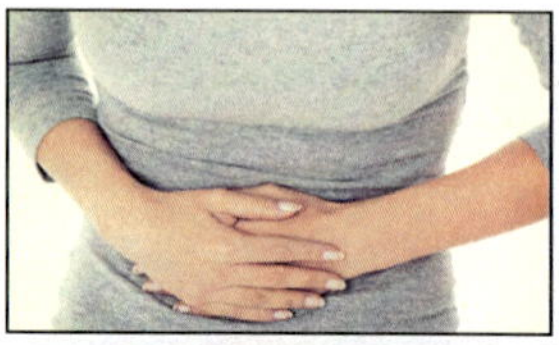

3. ____________

4. ____________

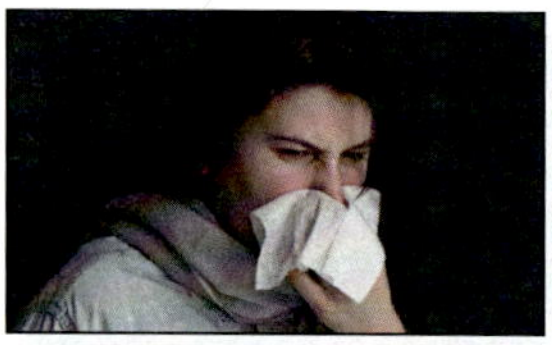

5. ____________

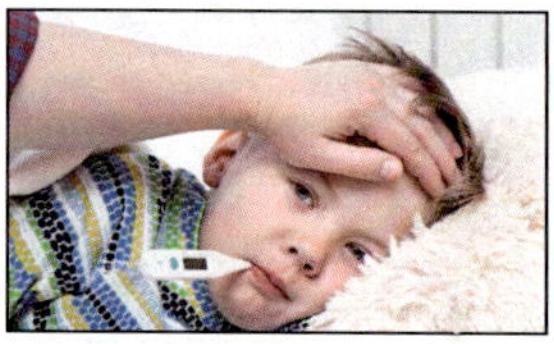

6. ____________

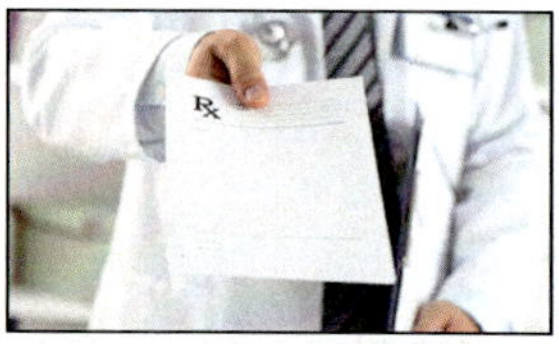

7. ____________

8. ____________

2 **Match the doctor's questions and statements with the patients' responses.**

Doctor	Patient
1. What symptoms have you noticed?	**a.** Oh! Then I definitely have a fever.
2. Do you have any allergies?	**b.** No, I've been vomiting since Monday.
3. I'll write you a prescription for that.	**c.** I've had a headache, sore throat, cough, and runny nose for two days.
4. Your temperature is almost 40 degrees Celsius!	**d.** Maybe the chicken I ate last night was bad.
5. You might have gotten food poisoning.	**e.** Yes, I haven't been able to eat fish or eggs since I was a child.
6. Have you been able to eat anything?	**f.** I don't like taking pills. Is there another way to cure it?

3 **Read the email. Circle the correct answers.**

Hey, Rose.
How are you doing? You must be very busy with your new medical practice. Congratulations, "Dr. cousin"! I (1 wasn't / haven't been) well lately. I wonder if I could ask you a few questions to see if I need to visit my doctor or not. My stomach (2 ached / has ached) since Saturday, but I don't know why. I (3 didn't eat / haven't eaten) anything strange on the weekend, so it can't be food poisoning. And I have no allergies. I also (4 vomited / have vomited) two times yesterday and (5 didn't keep / haven't kept) any food down since that time. I don't have any other symptoms. I (6 didn't have / haven't had) a fever, headache, cough, or sore throat at all. My mom (7 said / has said) that I should take some medicine, but you know I don't like to do that. What should I do? Help!

4 **Read Melissa's email again and put a check mark (✓) next to true or false.**

1. Melissa is having pain in her back. ☐ true ☐ false
2. She wants Rose to tell her what to do. ☐ true ☐ false
3. Melissa has had a fever and headaches. ☐ true ☐ false
4. Melissa wants to take pills as a cure. ☐ true ☐ false

Unit Review

A Email

Read Jessica's email. Then answer the questions.

Dear Becky,

Happy New Year! How are you? I've been good, but I'm busy at college. I joined the basketball team this year! We're actually fairly good. But being on the team is really tough. We practice three times a week and go to the gym twice a week. I started to lift weights and take yoga classes. Sometimes, I even go swimming. My schedule is pretty busy but quite fun, too. I also have a personal trainer. He will be helping me get in shape and teaching me to prepare a meal plan. It's cool that the school helps us with our fitness routine.

Some bad news: last week, I hurt my knee. It's still a little painful. My trainer recommended that I rest for a few days—which is okay with me! By the way, the Olympic basketball team will be visiting us next week! I'm pretty excited about that.

But enough about me. What will you be doing over the break?

Write back soon,
Jessica

1. What team did Jessica join at her college? ______________________
2. What does Jessica do at the gym? ______________________
3. What will her personal trainer be doing? ______________________
4. What happened last week? ______________________
5. What did her trainer recommend? ______________________
6. What is going to be happening next week? ______________________

B Write

Write an email back to Jessica on a separate piece of paper. Give your email to a partner to read and check. Then read your email out loud to the class.

C Reminder

Put a check mark (✓) next to the things you can do.

_______ Understand enough of what people say to be able to meet immediate needs

_______ Complete a simple questionnaire or standardized report form using short sentences

_______ Express yourself clearly in familiar, predictable situations

_______ Help solve practical problems by saying what you think and asking others what they think

Further Practice

A Prepare

Look at a person's fitness routine. Work with a partner. One of you is Person #1, and the other is Person #2. Look at your chart and cover the other chart. Ask your partner questions about each day and fill in the missing information in your chart. Pretend that today is Monday.

Person #1

Monday (TODAY)	Tuesday	Wednesday	Thursday	Friday	Saturday	Sunday
Gym: 30 minutes treadmill, lifting weights	Swimming: 30 minutes	Gym: 25 minutes yoga, lifting weights			Gym: 20 minutes treadmill, 20 minutes yoga	

Person #2

Monday (TODAY)	Tuesday	Wednesday	Thursday	Friday	Saturday	Sunday
Gym: 30 minutes treadmill, lifting weights			Rest	Basketball club		Gym: 20 minutes exercise bike, 20 minutes swimming

B Speak to Write

What do you think of the person's fitness routine? Do you have any suggestions or advice for him or her? With the same partner, discuss what you think he or she can change or add. Share your ideas with the class.

C Now Write

Write your own weekly fitness routine in the chart below. Then share it with another partner. What does your partner think of your routine? Next, ask your partner to make a meal plan for you. How does the meal plan help you reach your fitness goals?

		Monday	Tuesday	Wednesday	Thursday	Friday	Saturday	Sunday
Exercise Plan								
Meal Plan	(breakfast)							
	(lunch)							
	(dinner)							

MEMO

UNIT 7 Healthy Eating

Scan and find the tracks.

Before You Read

◆ **Talk about these questions with your classmates.**

1. Think of a supermarket product you usually buy. What brand is it?
2. How often do you try a different brand of this product?
3. Who is someone you know that enjoys trying new things? What new things does this person enjoy doing?

Vocabulary

◆ **Read the definitions. Then match each word in bold with its definition.**

A. a space with limits and certain characteristics
B. being shown or being in contact with
C. a way of behaving, thinking, or feeling that is not learned
D. a good feeling; a feeling of ease
E. the edge or end of how far something can go
F. to connect
G. an area; a part of a country
H. to make larger

1. ______ When you are too tired to keep going, push beyond your **limit**.

2. ______ People benefit from repeated **exposure** to new experiences.

3. ______ You can **expand** your tastes by trying new foods.

4. ______ Having a wider **comfort** zone leads to greater enjoyment of a variety of experiences.

5. ______ Humans and animals have a natural survival **instinct**.

6. ______ Some people are afraid to step out of their comfort **zone**.

7. ______ What kinds of food are from the country or **region** where you grew up?

8. ______ Choosing comfort foods over other foods is **linked** to our emotions.

Going Beyond the Familiar and Comfortable

Track 083

Comfort foods are the foods that you want and need when you are sad or sick. Such foods have no real power to make a person happy or feel better, so why do we choose certain ones?

One reason we choose a food as a comfort food is because it is familiar. Psychologists link this to our natural survival instinct. What we know has not hurt or killed us; thus, it is safe. What we don't know, on the other hand, might hurt or kill us; thus, it should be avoided.

Besides our natural instincts, we might also feel pride in certain comfort foods. The

Cheese Sandwich
bread, cheese, butter

Pasta
pasta, tomato, sauce, onion, garlic

Stew
beef, onions, potatoes, carrots

Tacos
tortilla, beef, lettuce, tomato, cheese

Chicken Noodle Soup
chicken, noodles, carrots, water

▲ Comfort foods are often made of simple things.

foods from the country or region of our childhoods are linked to our development. They are linked to our culture and beliefs. Of course these foods are better than others! Why eat anything else?

Too much reliance on what is familiar and comfortable, however, is not actually a benefit for us. People who step out of their comfort zones end up expanding them. True expansion comes from repeated exposure to new experiences. This is true with food as well. New foods or experiences become familiar and even enjoyable over time. Thus, a larger comfort zone leads to greater enjoyment of a wider range of experiences.

It is easy to push the limits of your comfort zone with food. Try preparing one of your favorite foods in a totally different way. Order something at your favorite restaurant that you have never tried before. Better yet, visit a restaurant you have never even been to. As the old saying goes, "Try it. You might like it!"

Review the Highlights

◆ **Mark up the text and infographic according to the instructions.**

1. Paragraphs 2 and 3 both list reasons why people choose certain comfort foods. Underline the reasons given in each paragraph.
2. Look at Paragraph 4. Underline the way a person can expand his or her comfort zone.
3. Look at Paragraph 4. Underline the benefit of expanding your comfort zone.
4. Look at Paragraph 5. Circle the author's suggestions for pushing the limits of your comfort zone.
5. Look at the infographic. What is the function of the infographic?

   Check your choice: ☐ comparing ☐ ranking ☐ labeling

Check Your Comprehension

◆ Circle the correct answer.

1. What is the passage mainly about? Main idea
   a. The healing power of food
   b. How foods change over time
   c. The best comfort foods
   d. The benefit of trying new things

2. How does a person expand his or her comfort zone with food? Details: what
   a. Having repeated exposure to new foods
   b. Linking foods with childhood experiences
   c. Living in regions with various food choices
   d. Recognizing what natural instinct is

3. Which is NOT an explanation for why we have certain comfort foods? Negative fact
   a. Culture b. Farming zones c. Pride d. Survival instinct

4. What is the key information shown in the infographic? Purpose
   a. Foods found in different regions
   b. New foods to expand one's comfort zone
   c. Healthy meal choices
   d. The simple ingredients of comfort foods

5. Which statement would the author probably agree with? Inference
   a. Comfort foods are the best foods for us.
   b. It is better to eat at home rather than to eat out.
   c. People with wider comfort zones enjoy life more.
   d. Restaurants limit our food choices.

◆ Complete the summary. Write the words from the reading that best fit in the blanks. One word is extra.

expand exposure instinct linked limits region comfort zone

People choose certain 1. ______________ foods because they are familiar. This is linked to a person's natural 2. ______________, or what they know will not harm them. People also consider some foods better than others because they are from the 3. ______________ where they grew up. The foods that are familiar to a person are also 4. ______________ to his or her culture and beliefs. However, people shouldn't rely too much on what is familiar and comfortable. They should 5. ______________ their 6. ______________ and enjoy new foods and experiences. True expansion comes from repeated 7. ______________ to new experiences. A wider comfort zone for both foods and experiences may lead to more enjoyment of life.

Linked Skills Activity

◆ **Look at the following types of foods. List two or three large restaurant chains that serve this kind of food. Then compare your ideas with a partner. Add any new restaurant names from your partner's list.**

Donuts	Hamburgers	Ice Cream	Pizza	Other Fast Foods

◆ **Read the information below. Fill in the blanks. Then compare your answers with a partner. Are your answers the same?**

Some restaurant chains can be found in just about any country. The foods served in these chains seem to grow in popularity year by year. Below is a list of some of the largest restaurant chains in the world. The name of each restaurant is not given. Can you guess it?

1. ______________: This hamburger chain first opened in the US in 1955. There are more than 34,000 of these restaurants around the world today. The restaurant is famous for its super-sized items.
2. ______________: This sandwich chain is famous for its long sandwiches, called "subs." Many people see the sandwiches as a healthy choice instead of a hamburger. Today, more than 28,000 of these restaurants can be found spread across 86 countries.
3. ______________: This fast food chain specializes in fried chicken and is the world's second largest restaurant chain. The first one opened in 1952 in the US, and today this chain has almost 19,000 restaurants in 118 countries.
4. ______________: This donut chain specializes in donuts and coffee, but they sell breakfast sandwiches and smoothies as well. The first of these restaurants opened in 1950 in the US. Today, the chain has more than 10,000 stores spread across 32 countries.
5. ______________: This fast food chain specializes in Mexican food. It is really Mexican food in a US style, but that does not stop a lot of people from loving it. There are almost six thousand of these restaurants around the world.

◆ **Your teacher will tell you the answers. After hearing them, discuss the following questions in small groups.**

1. Which of the restaurants in the reading operate in your country? How popular are they? Are other restaurants that serve the same food more popular?
2. What is a food from your country that people around the world enjoy or would enjoy? Which restaurant chains (if any) serve this food?

Keimyung's Millstones and *Doks:

Symbols of Learning and Patience

Track 084

[**KMU Core Competency:** Emotional Intelligence]

Millstones were once an essential tool in the daily lives of Koreans. In the past, nearly every household had a millstone to grind grains for family meals or special events. These tools were vital for preparing traditional foods, and today, they are important cultural symbols. At Keimyung University, millstones can be seen in several gardens, especially near the Dongsan Library on the Seongseo Campus and in the Stone Garden at the Daemyung Campus. These millstones represent the process of learning and growth. Just as grains must be carefully ground into fine flour, knowledge needs to be refined and processed to help students succeed in their studies and personal lives.

The *dok*, a traditional earthen pot, is another key part of Korean culture. These pots are used to ferment and preserve food, such as turning soybeans into soy sauce or cabbage into kimchi. They also store grains and water. *Doks* were especially important in the past, helping families preserve nutrients during harsh winters. Keimyung University features four *dok* gardens, which symbolize patience and transformation. Like fermentation, learning takes time—ideas must mature to reach their full potential and benefit others.

These symbols—millstones and *doks*—teach students valuable lessons about growth and reflection. They also promote **emotional intelligence** by encouraging students to embrace patience, adapt to challenges, and reflect on their learning. These qualities prepare students to grow into thoughtful and well-rounded individuals, ready to face the future.

**Doks*: Traditional Korean jars made of clay, designed for fermenting and storing food items such as soy sauce, soybean paste, and chili paste.

Check Your Comprehension

1. What does the millstone symbolize?

   (A) Grinding knowledge into something students can understand and use
   (B) Mixing ingredients to make tasty food
   (C) Competing to get good grades
   (D) Storing grains for later use

2. Which is NOT a function of the dok?

   (A) Fermenting vegetables
   (B) Storing small amounts of grain
   (C) Boiling rice
   (D) Preserving water for drinking

3. How many dok gardens are there at Keimyung?

   (A) 2
   (B) 4
   (C) 6
   (D) 8

Talk or Write about It

1. How can we prepare ourselves to process knowledge, like the millstone grinds grains?

   ____

   ____

2. How can we prepare to develop ideas over time, like the dok ferments food?

   ____

   ____

3. What qualities, like patience or reflection, can help us contribute to society?

   ____

   ____

7C The Doctor Said...

A Model Conversation

Read the conversation. Then listen. Track 085

Christa: Hey, how did it go at the clinic?

Adam: Not bad. It's my first checkup since I quit smoking. And I got good news—I'm in pretty good shape. I got a chest X-ray, and my lungs have already started healing.

Christa: That's great! Didn't you only quit two months ago?

Adam: Yeah, your lungs can start healing fast. I also asked for diet advice because I've gained a little weight since quitting. The doctor said to cut down on sugary and alcoholic drinks and to keep walking every day.

Christa: That makes sense. Did she tell you to do anything else?

Adam: Yeah, she actually told me to eat more fat! According to her, I'm eating too much bread and pasta. She said to cut down on those and eat more healthy fats, like fish and salads with olive oil.

Christa: I've heard that, too. They help you lose weight because you feel full for a long time after eating.

Adam: Right. Mmm, now I'm hungry. Let's go get some seafood and salad for lunch.

Brief note

Here, the word "fat" means the oily (liquid or solid) part of certain foods, like butter, nuts, and meat.

B Vocabulary

Listen to the conversation again. Then match the words with the correct definitions.

1. clinic	**a.** an examination by a doctor to check for medical problems
2. checkup	**b.** to get better after being hurt or damaged
3. diet	**c.** having a lot of sugar in it
4. lungs	**d.** a place to get medical help
5. heal	**e.** what a person eats; an eating plan for weight loss, better health, etc.
6. cut down on	**f.** having alcohol in it (for example, beer and wine)
7. sugary	**g.** a phrase used to say where some information came from
8. alcoholic	**h.** liquid fat from olives, which is a common part of Mediterranean diets
9. according to	**i.** the part of the body in the chest used for breathing
10. olive oil	**j.** to do or use less of (something)

C In Your World

Do you know anyone who is on a special diet? Who? (It can be you.) Why is this person on this diet? What should and shouldn't he or she eat? Tell a partner.

Should eat	Shouldn't eat

D Grammar

Reported speech with infinitives; *about* for topic

reported speech with *said* + (*not*) infinitive / *told* + object + (*not*) infinitive	
original	**reported**
"You need to get more exercise," the doctor said. "Don't arrive late," said Samantha. "Have another drink," Victor said (to me). "Don't lift too much weight," Gloria said (to her).	The doctor **said to get** more exercise. Samantha **said not to arrive** late. Victor **told me to have** another drink. Gloria **told her not to lift** too much weight.
reported speech with *talked about* / *told* + object + *about* to report the topic of a conversation	
"On our first date, we went to a movie." "I love nightclubs. There are many kinds…"	He **told me about** their first date. She **talked about** nightclubs.

Brief note

The verb *tell* always needs an indirect object that shows who the listener was. The verb *say* cannot have an indirect object in reported instructions, advice, or suggestions.

E Grammar Practice

Rewrite the sentences as reported speech. Use the given reporting verbs.

1. "Cut down on fast food," said Dr. Smith. (said)

____

2. "You should call the clinic and make an appointment," Karl said to his roommate. (told)

____

3. "I'm sorry," said the theater employee, "but you can't bring snacks into the theater." (said)

____

4. "I remember the night I met your father," Peter's mom said. "We danced and ate ice cream. We never wanted the night to end." (talked)

____

F Listen to Write

Listen to a short talk by a nutrition expert. On a separate sheet of paper, take notes on his advice. Compare your notes with a partner's. Track 086

Now write 4–5 sentences about the talk and the expert's advice.

Check Your Progress

1 **Circle the word that is different in each group.**

1. doctor / clinic / sugary / checkup
2. olive oil / X-ray / lungs / smoking

2 **Listen to the conversation and circle true or false.** Track 087

1.	The doctor told James to stop working out.	true	false
2.	James told the doctor that he eats too much fast food.	true	false
3.	The doctor said that some fats are healthy.	true	false
4.	James said he can't stop eating fast food.	true	false

3 **Listen again. Circle the correct answers.**

1. According to the (doctor / X-ray), James's lungs are healing nicely.
2. The doctor said James should also focus on (his diet / working out).
3. James said he eats fast food because (he's busy / he loves it).
4. The doctor told James to (quit eating / cut down on) fast food.
5. James said he (will / will try to) start eating better.

4 **Underline the errors. Rewrite the sentences correctly.**

1. Dr. Casey said me to cut down on alcoholic drinks. ______________________
2. According in the newspaper, it will raining tonight. ______________________
3. My friend told to us about his trip to China. ______________________
4. The book said walking every day. ______________________
5. The professor talked good fats and bad fats. ______________________

5 **Unscramble the words in the box. Then use them to fill in the blanks. Each word can only be used once.**

puckhec	slung	ahle	lincci	choocalli

1. Doctors advise us to get a ______________________ once a year.
2. We breathe with our ______________________.
3. How long will it take for my knee to ______________________, doctor?
4. Dr. Paz is opening a new ______________________.
5. ______________________ drinks can damage your body.

7D If You Want to Eat Healthily...

A Authentic Text: Health blog

Read the blog post. Then listen. Track 088

Brief note

"Calcium" (Ca) is a metal that people need for strong bones and teeth. It is found naturally in foods like milk and green vegetables.

If you're confused about how to eat right, you're not alone! Everyone recommends that you eat a balanced diet. But there is no *one* way to eat healthily. Everyone needs the same basic nutrients. But your size, physical activity, sex, and age all affect your dietary needs.

1. **Size and Physical Activity:** If you are tall and exercise a lot, you can eat more and not gain weight. For example, the actor and wrestler Dwayne ("The Rock") Johnson eats 5,000 calories a day. This includes three pounds of fish. But he's 195 centimeters tall and lifts weights six days a week. If your size is average and you don't exercise, you don't need as much food.
2. **Sex:** Men are bigger than women, so they need to eat more. If you are an active man weighing 175 pounds, you should eat about 2,800 calories a day. If you are an active woman weighing 125 pounds, you should eat about 2,000. Also, men need more protein to avoid losing muscle. Women need more calcium. If they don't get enough, their bones become weak and break more easily.
3. **Age:** If you're young, your body burns calories quickly. People's ability to burn calories slows down when they get older. It also becomes more difficult for their bodies to get vitamins from food. So if you're over 50, you should eat less, and you might need to take a daily vitamin pill.

Brief note

Here, "burn" means to use for energy. Your body *burns* the calories in food for energy.

B Vocabulary

Read the blog post again. Then match the words with the correct definitions.

1. calorie
2. pound
3. balanced
4. vitamin
5. sex
6. nutrients
7. average
8. bones

a. having a healthy mix of parts or a fair proportion of parts
b. something found naturally in food that is necessary for good health
c. a measurement of weight, equal to 0.45 kilogram
d. a measurement of the amount of energy in food
e. the usual or typical amount
f. the physical state of being either male, female, or intersex
g. one of the hard pieces that make the structure inside a person or animal
h. any substance that animals need to eat and plants need from the soil in order to live and grow

C Comprehension

Choose the correct answers.

1.	What is special about Dwayne Johnson's diet?	a. He eats a lot of calories.		b. He only eats fish.
2.	Who should eat more calories, on average?	a. women	b. men	c. older people
3.	What do women need more of than men?	a. vitamins	b. protein	c. calcium
4.	What do men need more of than women?	a. vitamins	b. protein	c. calcium
5.	Who might need to take a daily vitamin pill?	a. young people	b. women	c. older people

D In Your World

Make a list of foods you usually eat. Discuss your list with a partner. Which foods do you think are healthy and unhealthy? How does eating these foods make you feel?

E Grammar

Zero conditional

Zero conditional sentences are *if* sentences about general facts in the present. Both clauses are in the simple present. The result clause may or may not begin with *then*.		
	condition	**result**
If	you **exercise** a lot, you**'re** young, they **have** a big lunch, people **don't eat**,	(then) you **can eat** more. (then) your body **burns** calories quickly. (then) they **feel** tired in the afternoon. (then) they **get** hungry.

Brief note

You can switch the order of the clauses:
Your body burns calories quickly if you're young.

F Grammar Practice

Put the words in order to make sentences. Try writing the sentences again with the clauses in a different order.

1. feel / if / fat / eat / you / you / full

______________________________.

2. unhealthy / weight / too / if / gain / you / become / you / much

______________________________.

3. I / healthy / eat / plenty / have / if / energy / of / I / food

______________________________.

4. weak / if / don't / bones / women's / they / calcium / eat / become

______________________________.

G Use the Language

Travel advice

Work in small groups. Imagine a traveler is coming from a foreign country. Discuss what advice you would give him or her about eating and drinking in your country. Write your advice in complete sentences and share it with other groups. Are your lists similar or different? In what ways?

____

____

____

____

____

Check Your Progress

1 Match the example on the left with a word on the right.

1. B12 ______ a. balanced
2. male ______ b. average
3. meat, fruit, vegetables ______ c. calories
4. 150 per serving ______ d. vitamin
5. 70 percent ______ e. sex

2 Fill in the blanks to spell words that match the pictures.

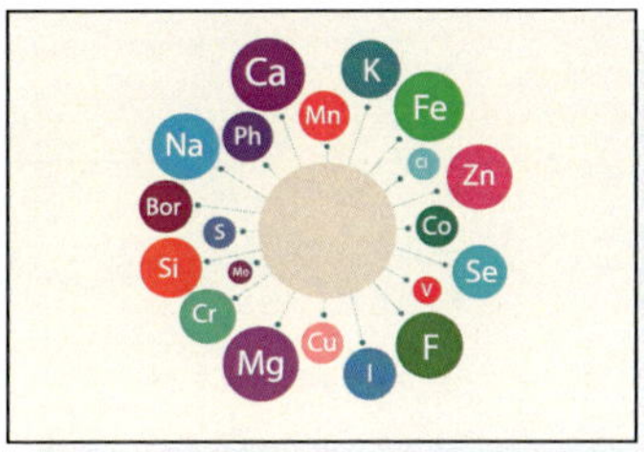

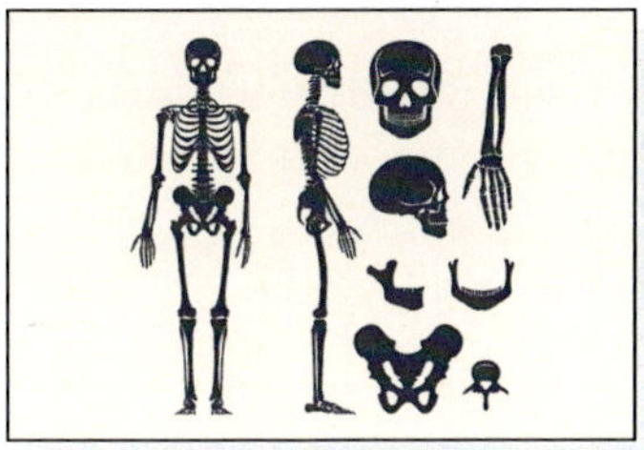

1. n __ __ r __ __ n t __ 2. __ o __ e __ 3. p __ __ __ d s

3 Match each condition with the correct result.

1. If women don't get enough calcium, • • a. you gain a lot of weight.
2. Men lose muscle • • b. he does not need to eat as much food.
3. If you eat too many calories, • • c. their bones become weak and could break more easily.
4. If John doesn't exercise often, • • d. if you're an active woman weighing 125 pounds.
5. You should get 2,000 calories a day • • e. if they don't get enough protein.

4 Circle the correct answers.

1. If you're young, your body (is burning / burns) calories more quickly.
2. Your body's ability to burn calories (slows / slowed) down if you are older than 50.
3. If you (are / were) active, you need more calories.
4. You will gain weight if you (do eat / eat) too much.

5 Rewrite each sentence using the zero conditional.

1. Eating a balanced diet is the best way to stay healthy.
   If you ____.
2. People who exercise a lot can eat more food without gaining weight.
   If you ____.
3. People who are more than 50 years old need less food but might need vitamin pills.
   If you are ______________________________________.

7E I'm a Vegetarian

A Model Conversation

Read the conversation. Then listen. Track 089

Mike: Hey, Julia, would you like a **steak**? They're almost ready.

Julia: Actually, I brought some vegetables to grill. I'm a vegetarian.

Mike: Really? Wow. Was it hard to stop eating meat?

Julia: It was at first, but it's been two years, and I've never felt better.

Mike: That's good, but I read an article recently. It said that people need meat to get enough protein and a certain vitamin. I forget which one.

Julia: It's vitamin B12. Well, there's protein in eggs and **beans**, so I eat those a lot. And eggs have vitamin B12, too.

Mike: I see. Why did you stop eating meat, if you don't mind my asking?

Julia: At first, it was for weight loss. Then my doctor told me vegetarians have less **risk** of heart **disease** and **cancer**.

Mike: Well, I still can't live without meat. Steak is so delicious, and vegetables are so **bland**.

Julia: They're not if you know how to cook them! You just need the right **spices** and **recipes**.

Brief note

A "vegetarian" is a person who does not eat any meat. *Vegetarian* can also be an adjective: *vegetarian recipes.*

B Vocabulary

Listen to the conversation again. Then fill in the blanks with the bold words from the conversation.

1. My mom keeps all her favorite ______________ in a box in the kitchen.
2. If you don't brush your teeth twice a day, you have a higher ______________ of cavities.
3. I'd like to order the grilled ______________, but it's so expensive. I'd better get the chicken.
4. Chili and cinnamon are common ______________ that are used in everyday cooking.
5. People often eat ______________ with rice.
6. If you have nausea or a stomachache, you should only eat ______________ foods.
7. Smoking is dangerous. Smokers have a high risk of getting lung ______________.
8. Cancer is a serious ______________. Millions of people die from it each year.

C In Your World

Work with a partner. Make a list of foods that have lots of protein, a list of bland foods, and a list of any vitamins and other nutrients that you know. Compare your list with another pair's. Discuss the differences.

Foods with Protein	Bland Foods	Vitamins and Other Nutrients

D Grammar

Reported speech with *that* clauses

To report past statements that are still true, use a past tense reporting verb (for example, *said*) with a simple present verb in the reported speech: subject + *said* (*that*) + clause; subject + *told* + object + (*that*) + clause

original	reported
"Vegetables are so bland," he said.	He **said that** vegetables are bland.
"You shouldn't eat before dinner," Mom said (to me).	Mom **told me that** I shouldn't eat before dinner.
"Vegetarians have a lower risk of developing cancer," the doctor said (to me).	The doctor **told me** vegetarians have a lower risk of developing cancer.

Brief note

In conversation, the word *that* can be left out: *He said vegetables are bland.*

E Grammar Practice

In each reported past statement, one word is missing or incorrect. Underline the mistake. Then write the correct word or the missing word.

1. The doctor said me that I should eat more vegetables. ____________
2. She saying that you don't get enough vitamin C. ____________
3. I told he shouldn't drink so much alcohol. ____________
4. The article said that there was protein in beans. ____________
5. Yesterday Sam tells me my diet isn't healthy. ____________

Rewrite each sentence as reported speech.

6. "There are great recipes online," he said.

____

7. "Eggs have important nutrients," the professor said to us.

____

8. "It's not hard to eat a vegetarian diet," the doctor said to me.

____

F Use the Language

Where should we eat?

Go online and look up reviews of nearby restaurants. Find one that you like or would like to try. Then write four sentences reporting what you read.

Now get in groups and decide where your group will eat tonight. Try to convince your partners that your place is the best based on your research.

1.
2.
3.
4.

Check Your Progress

1 **Match the words with their definitions.**

1. risk	______	**a.** cooking directions	
2. cancer	______	**b.** chance of something happening	
3. steak	______	**c.** plain; not tasty	
4. bland	______	**d.** a type of disease	
5. recipe	______	**e.** beef	

2 **Fill in the blanks with the correct words from the box. Use each word only once.**

beans	spices	disease	vegetarian	protein

Because they don't eat meat, ❶ ______________s need to be sure they get enough ❷ ______________ in their diets. They can get this in foods such as ❸ ______________, eggs, and nuts. Many people don't love the taste of vegetables, but vegetarians use special recipes and ❹ ______________ to make delicious dishes. Nutritionists say that vegetarians have less risk for cancer and other serious ❺ ______________s.

3 **Match the reported speech with the original.**

1. The woman told the boys that they should slow down. •

2. The doctor said that I'm at risk for heart disease. •

3. Frank told her that she shouldn't eat so much sugar. •

• **a.** "Is that candy? Donna, you've got to cut down on sugary snacks," he said.

• **b.** "You could have heart problems if you don't start eating healthy," he said.

• **c.** "Jorge! Dan! Don't run at the swimming pool," she shouted. "You could slip and fall."

4 **Put a check mark (✓) next to the correct sentence with the same meaning.**

1. "At your age, your body needs more protein and less fat," the doctor said.

☐ The doctor said that I should eat more protein. ☐ The doctor said that I'm too fat.

2. Henry told Debra that she needs to get more exercise.

☐ "Debra is exercising a lot more these days," Henry said.

☐ "You should go to the gym more often, Debra," said Henry.

3. "Eggs have lots of vitamin B12, which vegetarians need," she said.

☐ She said that vegetarians need vitamin B12. ☐ She said that vegetarians eat eggs.

4. He said that vegetables taste bland.

☐ "Vegetables are delicious," he said. ☐ "Vegetables are tasteless," he said.

7F What Does It Say on the Label?

A Model Conversation

Read the conversation. Then listen. Track 090

Nutrition Facts

Serving Size		52 g
Amount Per Serving		
Calories 150	Calories from Fat	45
		% Daily Value*
Total Fat 5 g		8%
Saturated Fat 5 g		8%
Trans Fat 0 g		0%
Cholesterol 0 mg		0%
Sodium 100 mg		4%
Total Carbohydrate 38 g		13%
Dietary Fiber less than 1 g		3%
Sugars 17 g		
Protein 2 g		
Vitamin A 0% • Vitamin C 0% • Calcium 0% • Iron 4%		

INGREDIENTS: WHOLE GRAIN WHEAT, SUGAR, RICE, WHEAT BRAN, BROWN SUGAR SYRUP, SOLUBLE WHEAT FIBER, CONTAINS 2% OR LESS OF SALT, MALT FLAVORING, STRAWBERRY FLAVORING

Marta: We need breakfast food. Ooh, this cereal looks good.

Jill: Strawberry Crunch? Let me see the box. Craig, my personal trainer, says people should read the label on everything. Oh, look at the ingredients: wheat, sugar—sugar is second!

Marta: A little sugar isn't so bad. It only has 150 calories per serving. Plus, I love strawberries.

Jill: But this cereal doesn't have real strawberries, just strawberry flavor. And it's not nutritious at all. See? The label says there are no vitamins, no calcium...

Marta: Okay, put it back. What do you suggest we get for breakfast?

Jill: Let's get some fresh strawberries, or frozen ones. And some yogurt. We can put them in the blender and make smoothies.

Marta: Okay, but there's yogurt in our fridge already. By the way, what does Craig say about frozen fruits?

Jill: He tells me they're usually as nutritious as fresh ones.

Brief note

A "smoothie" is a fruit drink made by mixing the ingredients in a blender.

B Vocabulary

Listen to the conversation again. Choose the correct answers.

1. An **ingredient** is ______. a. a type of prepared food b. one part of a prepared food
2. A **frozen** food is ______. a. very cold b. very bland
3. A **serving** of a food is ______. a. the amount you buy b. the amount to eat at one time
4. **Nutritious** foods are ______. a. healthy b. expensive

C In Your World

Work with a partner. Look at the foods below. Make guesses about their nutrition facts. Then find real nutrition labels for these foods online. How close were your guesses? Compare with another pair of students.

pancakes	Ingredients: ______ Calories per serving: ______ Sugar per serving: ____ g (grams)	**vanilla ice cream**	Ingredients: ______ Calories per serving: ______ Fat per serving: ____ g (grams)

D Grammar

Reported speech with simple present tense

Use a reporting verb in the simple present to report things that people have often said, opinions that people still hold, and things that are currently written on signs, labels, etc.: subject + *say/says* (*that*) + clause; subject + *tell/tells* + object + (*that*) + clause

original	reported
"Yogurt is good for breakfast," she says to me.	She **tells me (that)** yogurt is good for breakfast.
"People should read labels," Craig often says.	Craig often **says (that)** people should read labels.
Calcium 0%	The label **says (that)** there's no calcium.

E Grammar Practice

Rewrite the sentences as reported speech. Use the correct form of the verbs in the simple present.

1. Fresh fruit is too expensive, according to Alan. (say)

   ____

2. "Athletes need to drink lots of water," Dr. Garcia often says to his patients. (tell)

   ____

3. You can't park here, according to the sign. (say)

   ____

4. "Many women don't get enough vitamin D," Isabella says to me. (tell)

   ____

5. "Fruit juice can have as much sugar in it as soda," Franklin often explains to his kids. (tell)

   ____

F Read to Speak

Work with a partner. Each of you read one of the paragraphs below. Tell each other what you read.

Kale, sometimes called "the king of green vegetables," is one of the healthiest foods in the world. One cup of kale contains 14 important vitamins and nutrients. Eating kale is a fantastic way to increase the amount of nutrients in your diet. Kale has lots of vitamin C. This vitamin helps our bodies fight many diseases. Kale also has several nutrients that help prevent cancer and heart disease. It has nutrients that can help you lose weight, see better, and live longer, too. So add some kale to your diet today. You'll be glad you did!

Acai is a berry found in the rainforests of the Amazon. It is often praised for its health benefits. Acai is high in vitamin C, which boosts a person's immune system and even helps prevent cancer. Some people think acai berries help them lose weight. People who regularly have a handful of acai berries also think it decreases exhaustion and gives them more energy throughout the day.

Check Your Progress

1 Complete the crossword.

Across →

1. amount of food
4. a part of prepared food
6. a cold place to keep food

Down ↓

2. healthy
3. mixing machine
5. very cold food

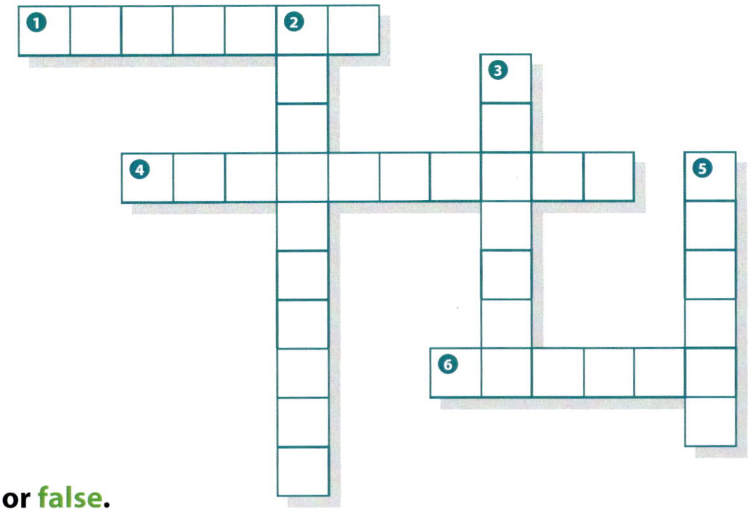

2 Read the label and circle true or false.

Nutrition Facts

Serving Size	22 g
Amount Per Serving	
Calories 110 Calories from Fat 30	
	% Daily Value*
Fat 5g	6%
Total Carbohydrate 17 g	13%
Fiber 1 g	7%
Sugars 8 g	
Protein 2 g	0%
• Vitamin A 0% • Iron 8%	
• Vitamin C 0% • Calcium 0%	

Peanut Butter Crunchies

1. There are 110 calories in a serving of Peanut Butter Crunchies. true false
2. One serving is 22 grams. true false
3. There are 30 calories from fat in each serving. true false
4. This food has lots of protein. true false
5. This food is a good source of vitamin A. true false

3 Underline the errors. Rewrite the sentences correctly.

1. She always telling me that I should buy fresh fruit. ______________________
2. The signs said that we can't park here. ______________________
3. Allen tells to us that you're a vegetarian. ______________________
4. The label is saying there is 10 percent fat. ______________________

4 Write a reported speech sentence using the correct form of the given verb.

1. "You can't win if you don't play," my teacher always says to us. (tell)

____.

2. According to Rita, coffee is healthy. (say)

____.

3. "Men can continue to lift weights after age 40," Doctor Gordon advises. (say)

____.

4. "Kids, remember to read the labels when you shop," my mother says. (tell)

____.

7G If You Cook Them Too Long...

A Authentic Text: Recipe

Read the recipe.

Chicken with Broccoli and Red Pepper

Ingredients: 1 pound of chicken, 2 cups of rice, 1 cup of broccoli, 1 red pepper, 2 tablespoons of soy sauce, 2 tablespoons of olive oil

Directions:

1. Combine the rice with 4 cups of water in a saucepan. If you use less water, you will have drier rice. Put the saucepan on the stove on high heat. When the water is boiling, reduce the heat and let it cook for 20 minutes.
2. Chop the chicken and vegetables into small pieces. Stir-fry them with the olive oil and then quickly remove them from the stove. Check that the chicken is cooked through and not raw on the inside. Be careful, though. If you cook them too long, they will burn.
3. When the rice is cooked, combine it with the chicken and vegetables. Add seasoning and soy sauce. Enjoy this healthy dish!

Brief note

Sometimes the "directions" in a recipe are called the method.

B Vocabulary: Cooking

Match the words with the correct definitions.

1. combine	**a.** to make lower
2. reduce	**b.** uncooked
3. seasoning	**c.** to put together
4. raw	**d.** to take away; to take off
5. remove	**e.** something (such as salt, spices, or herbs) that is added to improve the taste of food

C About You

Tell a partner how to make a dish you know how to cook. As you talk, your partner writes the recipe. Then switch roles.

Name of dish: ______________________

Ingredients: ______________________

____

Directions: ______________________

____

D Grammar

First conditional

First conditional sentences are *if* sentences about the future. The *if* clause is in the simple present, and the result clause is in the future tense with *will/won't*. The result clause may or may not begin with *then*.

	condition	result
If	you **don't eat** enough nutrients, you **cook** the vegetables too long, we **eat** a lot of broccoli, I **keep** lifting weights,	(then) you **will get** sick. (then) they **will burn**. (then) we'**ll get** enough vitamin C. (then) I **won't be** weak.

Brief note

You can switch the order of the clauses:
I won't be weak if I keep lifting weights.

E Grammar Practice

Fill in the blanks with your own ideas to make true first conditional sentences.

1. If I am late for my next class, ______________________________.

2. ______________________________, I won't have much energy.

3. If you don't eat enough protein, ______________________________.

4. ______________________________, you'll gain weight.

5. If you start cooking all your meals at home, ______________________________.

6. ______________________________ if I never eat meat again.

7. If you eat at fast-food restaurants often, ______________________________.

8. ______________________________, you will get sick.

F Use the Language

If you eat our product…

Work in small groups. Create an advertisement for a food or drink. It can be a real food or drink or your own idea. Include some information about its ingredients, instructions for preparing it, and its effects on people's health.

Now take turns "selling" your product to the rest of the class.

Check Your Progress

1 **Circle the word that is different in each group.**

1. tablespoon / raw / cup

2. broccoli / pepper / saucepan

2 **Write a short definition for each word.**

1. combine ______________________

2. remove ______________________

3. reduce ______________________

4. seasoning ______________________

3 **Read the email. Then complete each sentence using *will/won't*.**

From: candy312@fastmail.com
To: collegeboy18@edu.com

Hi, Danny.

How do you like college so far? I hope you are getting enough to eat. I remember how tired you get when you don't. I also hope you're not eating a lot of snacks and fast food. You can save money by cooking for yourself, and it's much healthier! This website has delicious recipes that are fast and easy to make: www.quikmeals.com. Check it out.

You'll have to cook for yourself because no one else will do it for you. I know that it seems like a lot of work; it's much easier to go to Hamburger Haven. But I think the more often you do it, the more you will like it. Your father and I are taking a cooking class, and we're having so much fun! Tonight, Dad made steak with garlic seasoning and grilled peppers. It was delicious!

We hope to come see you before the end of the semester. Will you cook us dinner? I'll bring your favorite dessert if you do: homemade chocolate chip cookies!

Love,
Mom

1. If Danny doesn't get enough sleep, ______________________.

2. If Danny cooks for himself, ______________________.

3. If Danny doesn't cook for ______________________.

4. If Danny cooks more often, ______________________.

5. If Danny cooks dinner for his parents, ______________________.

4 **Listen to the conversations and match each one to the correct picture.** Track 091

1. __________

2. __________

3. __________

Unit Review

A These are healthy cookies!

Listen to a conversation at a supermarket. Fill in the blanks with the words that you hear. Then answer the questions. Track 092

Susie: Let's see. We have vegetables, chicken, fish, __________ __________... What else do we need?
Lucas: How about these cookies? Just a small box.
Susie: We really shouldn't, Lucas. The doctor said __________ __________ eating sweet snacks, remember?
Lucas: Yeah, but these are *healthy* cookies! The __________ __________ they don't have much fat and only 100 __________ per serving.
Susie: What's the first __________ on the list?
Lucas: Well, it's sugar.
Susie: See? We've worked so hard to lose weight and get __________ __________. If we start buying cookies, __________ go back to our bad old __________.
Lucas: You're right. We'd better not.
Susie: Don't look so sad. I know you miss __________, but we can get something tasty to cook for dinner. My sister gave me a __________ for Mexican rice and __________. She said it's __________.
Lucas: Okay, where are the beans?

1. What does Lucas want to buy? ____________________
2. What did their doctor tell them? ____________________
3. What did Susie's sister say about the recipe for rice and beans? ____________________

____

B Role-play

Pretend to shop for food with a partner. Find a grocery advertisement on your phone or in a newspaper. Use language from the unit to discuss what to buy and what not to buy. List the foods below.

SHOPPING LIST		
	1. __________	5. __________
	2. __________	6. __________
	3. __________	7. __________
	4. __________	8. __________

C Reminder

Put a check mark (✓) next to the things you can do.

__________ Understand the main points of clear, standard speech on familiar, everyday subjects
__________ Handle everyday situations such as shopping, making appointments, or checking appointment times
__________ Give practical instructions on how to do something (for example, cooking)

Further Practice

A Read to Write

Read part of a talk about nutrition. Then circle the correct words and fill in the blanks to complete the sentences.

"People get most of their protein from meat and cheese. Every person needs a different amount of protein each day. Young children need less protein, and people who work out and play sports need more. But everyone needs protein. Without it, you won't have strong bones and muscles."

Rebecca Beare, M.D.

1. The doctor (said / told) that every person ________________ a different amount of protein.
2. According to the doctor, if people (won't / don't) get enough protein, ________________ ________________.

B Speak to Write

Work with a partner. Practice saying the sentences below, taking turns filling in the blanks with your own words. How many different ways can you think of to complete each sentence?

1. He needs to stop smoking. If he doesn't quit, ________________.
2. If you always eat at restaurants, ________________.
3. My doctor tells me that ________________.

C Now Write

Read the paragraph. Then write a summary (a statement of the most important information) in your own words in ten minutes or less.

Making small changes in your diet can make a big difference. Experts on nutrition advise people to fill half of their plates at each meal with fruits and vegetables. That's a good way to start. People should also eat less salt and sugar because they increase the risk of heart disease and other illnesses. To begin cutting down on unhealthy snacks, drink one less soda and eat one less sweet or salty snack each day. Learning to eat healthily is like learning to walk. If you take one small step at a time, you'll soon be running!

____

____

____

MEMO

UNIT 8

City Life

Scan and find the tracks.

Before You Read

◆ **Talk about these questions with your classmates.**

1. Which color in the picture do you like the most?
2. Why do you like it the most?
3. How does it make you feel?

Vocabulary

◆ **Read the definitions. Then match each word in bold with its definition.**

A. supporting something or someone for a long time
B. to cause to like or be interested in something
C. a large building with many different shops inside
D. a feeling
E. tight; not flexible; unable to stretch
F. safe; protected
G. the feeling that something is very important and needs immediate attention
H. a small folding case that holds money, credit cards, etc.

1. ______ Different colors can bring out certain **emotions** in us.

2. ______ The color blue can make shoppers feel **loyal** to stores.

3. ______ **Malls** are very colorful places.

4. ______ Stores try to get shoppers to open their **wallets**.

5. ______ The color pink makes people feel calm and relaxes **tense** muscles.

6. ______ Some colors are known to make people feel **secure**.

7. ______ Red **attracts** customers, but it may also make them feel tense.

8. ______ The color red is related to a sense of **urgency**.

Do Colors Make You Spend More?

Track 093

If you walk into any mall, you will notice a rainbow of different colors. It is well known that colors affect our emotions. Stores often use this knowledge to influence how shoppers spend their money. In fact, there are even experts who help stores use color to make people spend more.

Experts have taught stores a variety of ways to get shoppers to open their wallets. Black makes things look classy. Many makeup products are packaged in black so that shoppers who buy them will feel special. Purple reminds people of royalty, and it is also used to package beauty products. It makes the buyer believe the item is important.

Other colors make people feel safe. For example, blue makes people feel secure.

GREEN
- Health
- Tranquility
- Money
- Nature

Workers in green environments have fewer stomach aches.

PURPLE
- Royalty
- Wealth
- Success
- Wisdom

Many kings wore purple robes.

PINK
- Calm
- Love
- Romance

"Drunk-tank pink" is a color used in prisons to calm inmates.

BROWN
- Reliability
- Boredom
- Practicality
- Earth

Many police and military uniforms feature the color brown.

ORANGE
- Excitement
- Enthusiasm
- Warmth
- Caution

Also used to draw attention to signs

WHITE
- Purity
- Innocence
- Empty
- Spacious

Great for creating the illusion of space

▲ What colors make us feel or think about

This is why many banks have blue logos. It also makes customers more loyal. White is similar. It brings out feelings of honesty and purity.

Pink makes people feel calm. It is known to help relax tense muscles. Red, however, has the opposite reaction. Although red may attract customers, it is related to a sense of urgency. This is why many clearance sale signs are red.

Bright colors, such as green and orange, have positive effects on people. Green makes people think about nature and doing good things for the planet. Orange makes shoppers feel that something is a good value. Fast food logos are often orange because buyers feel they are getting more food for their money.

No matter where you shop, it is important to be aware before opening your wallet. By knowing how colors are used, people can prevent stores from controlling how they spend their money.

Review the Highlights

◆ **Mark up the text and infographic according to the instructions.**

1. Look at Paragraph 1. Underline what thing stores use to influence people to spend their money.
2. Look at Paragraph 2. Circle what purple makes buyers believe.
3. Look at Paragraph 3. Underline what color banks use for their logos.
4. Look at the infographic. Besides calm, circle two other emotions people relate with pink.
5. Look at the infographic. Underline what people think of when they see green.

Check Your Comprehension

◆ **Circle the correct answer.**

1. How do experts help stores bring in more money? Details: how
   a. They package products in red.
   b. They use color to influence how shoppers spend money.
   c. They help customers feel calm.
   d. They make buyers feel like they are getting more for their money.

2. Why does white make people feel more loyal? Details: why
   a. Because it makes people feel calm
   b. Because it makes people feel classy
   c. Because it brings out feelings of honesty
   d. Because it brings out a sense of urgency

3. What is the reading about? Main idea
   a. Colors that make people feel safe and calm
   b. Why many clearance sale signs are red
   c. How color affects what people do and how they feel
   d. Different ways to get shoppers to open their wallets

4. According to the text, which color is NOT always related to a positive emotion? Negative fact
   a. Pink b. White c. Black d. Red

5. Based on the reading, how can you keep from spending money? Main situation
   a. Be aware that black can make you feel special.
   b. Only buy clearance items.
   c. Be aware of how stores use color to make you open your wallet.
   d. Do not go into stores with blue logos.

◆ **Complete the summary. Write the words from the reading that best fit in the blanks. One word is extra.**

tense attract wallets mall emotions loyal urgency secure

When you go to a 1. ______________, you will see many different colors. These colors can change your 2. ______________. Experts know how to use colors to get shoppers to open their 3. ______________. Banks use colors, such as blue, that make people feel 4. ______________ and 5. ______________. Pink makes people feel less 6. ______________. Red can make people feel a sense of 7. ______________. Experts know that people are attracted to certain colors. However, it is up to you to know how to prevent stores from controlling how you spend your money.

Linked Skills Activity

◆ **Work with a partner. Ask your partner which emotions he or she associates with each color. Next, discuss the stores, brands, and logos that use those colors. Switch roles.**

Color	**Emotions** - How do these colors make you feel?	**Stores/Brands/Logos** - Which stores, brands, or logos use these colors?
Red		
Orange		
Yellow		
Green		
Blue		
Purple		
Pink		
White		
Black		

◆ **Discuss the following questions with your partner.**

1. What is your favorite color? What was your favorite color as a child? Has your favorite color changed as you have gotten older? Why do you think that is?
2. Is there a color you hate? If so, what is it? Why do you hate it?

◆ **Choose one of the topics below. Write a paragraph about it.**

1. Do you think different cultures have different meanings for colors? What do the different colors mean in your culture? Provide examples to support your answer.

___

___

___

2. What colors are in your country's flag? What do the colors represent?

___

___

___

Student Culture Week at Keimyung University

Track 094

[KMU Core Competency: Communicative Ability]

Every year, Keimyung University hosts Student Culture Week, a vibrant event packed with cultural and artistic activities led by students. This event is carefully planned by the Student Council, the Association of Clubs, and the councils of each college. Together, they create programs that reflect the year's theme, making the week more than just a school festival. It connects the university to the local community and proudly showcases Keimyung's unique culture and identity.

The week offers a wide variety of events for students and visitors to enjoy. One highlight is the main concert, where well-known singers perform, filling the campus with energy and excitement. Students can also take part in a singing competition, showing off their talents and cheering on their friends. Other activities include public awareness campaigns about important issues like anti-smoking, blood donation, and safety. Traditional Korean culture is on display through a Taekwondo demonstration, while music students deliver a moving classical concert. For those who prefer outdoor activities, a group walk along Keimyung's scenic paths provides a relaxing way to connect with nature.

Student Culture Week also gives students the chance to improve their **communicative ability**. By planning and participating in these events, they learn to express ideas, collaborate with others, and build meaningful connections with the community.

This special week strengthens the bond between students, faculty, and locals, creating lasting memories and celebrating Keimyung's spirit of togetherness.

Check Your Comprehension

1. Who organizes Student Culture Week at Keimyung University?
   (A) Only the professors
   (B) The Student Council and other student groups
   (C) Local community leaders
   (D) The university's music department

2. What is one popular event during Student Culture Week?
   (A) A math competition
   (B) A cooking class
   (C) A soccer match with local teams
   (D) A main concert with famous singers

3. What is one purpose of Student Culture Week?
   (A) To make students study harder
   (B) To teach students how to sing
   (C) To build connections with the community
   (D) To promote only classical music

Talk or Write about It

1. What part of Korean culture would you like to share with others?

   ____

   ____

2. What valuable skills can students gain by organizing cultural events?

   ____

   ____

3. What makes a student cultural event successful?

   ____

   ____

Shopping Trips

8C The Best Shopping in Town

A Authentic Text: Shopping guide

Read part of a tourist information brochure about shopping in San Francisco. Which of these places would you most like to visit?

> **Brief note**
>
> A *vendor* is a seller. "Street vendors" are people who sell things outside on the street rather than inside a building.

SAN FRANCISCO SHOPPING GUIDE

3 Chinatown
Not far from North Beach, there's a little piece of China. You will feel like you're in Shanghai as you explore shops with a huge selection of imports, from furniture to tea. From the area's many street vendors, you can also pick up fun souvenirs and some delicious but inexpensive Chinese cuisine.

1 North Beach
Don't miss out on San Francisco's well-known Italian district, with an *Italiano* style that you can see and taste! Visit fashionable shops offering clothing, accessories, and home décor. And when you're done, enjoy authentic Italian food at one of the many fine restaurants in the area.

2 Union Square
This downtown district is the number-one destination for both local shoppers and tourists. Shop around for men's and women's clothing, accessories, beauty products, electronics, and more. If you ever get tired of shopping, you can check out some of Union Square's many theaters, art galleries, salons, or hotels.

B Vocabulary

Match the words and phrases with the correct definitions.

1. accessory	**a.** brought from one country to another for sale
2. electronics	**b.** a certain area or neighborhood in a city
3. get tired of	**c.** something you buy to remember a place you visited
4. district	**d.** a number of different choices
5. genuine	**e.** products that use electricity, such as TVs, computers, cell phones, etc.
6. fashionable	**f.** cooking; food
7. selection	**g.** something you wear besides clothes, such as a hat, a scarf, a bag, etc.
8. imported	**h.** showing taste and style (in clothes, hair, etc.) that is popular now
9. souvenir	**i.** real; true; not copied or false
10. cuisine	**j.** to become bored or impatient with (something)

C About You

Think of the last time you visited a popular shopping area. What was it like? Did you buy anything? Tell a partner, and answer his or her questions. Listen to your partner's experience and ask questions.

D Grammar

Phrasal verbs

Brief note

Inseparable phrasal verbs may be transitive (having a direct object) or intransitive. All separable phrasal verbs are transitive.

phrasal verbs		
Phrasal verbs are made up of a verb plus one or more particles (words that look like prepositions or adverbs): for example, *hang out*. Phrasal verbs are most common in informal speech and writing. There are two main types: inseparable and separable.		
	examples	**sentences**
inseparable There is no object between the verb and the particle(s).	*hang out, drop by, get around, shop around (for), miss out (on), log in/out, sign in/out*	Let's **hang out** at the mall. Don't **miss out on** this amazing sale. I want to **shop around for** phones before I buy one. **Drop by** our store to get a great deal on shoes.
separable The object may come between the verb and the particle.	*turn on/off, pick up, think over, throw away, look up, find out, check out, put on, take off, drop off*	Did you **pick up** some school supplies? Did you **pick** them **up**? We should **check** Chinatown **out** before we go. We should **check** it **out** before we go.

Brief note

When the object is a personal pronoun, it must come between the verb and the particle.
(✓) *Pick it up.* (X) *Pick up it.*

E Grammar Practice

Fill in the blanks with one of the phrasal verbs from above. Use a dictionary to help you if necessary.

1. My mom used to ______________ me ______________ at school every morning.
2. I'm going to ______________ my shoes ______________ because they're uncomfortable.
3. It's getting cold. You should ______________ ______________ your sweater.
4. If you don't come to the party, you'll ______________ ______________ ______________ a fun evening.

Underline the error and write the correct phrase. If the sentence is correct, write *correct*.

5. I didn't know the meaning of this word, so I looked up it. ____________________
6. He uses the subway to get town around. ____________________
7. No one is watching TV, so please turn off it. ____________________
8. My parents are out of town. Want to hang it out? ____________________

F Use the Language

Partners in business

Working in pairs or small groups, pick a business, store, or restaurant that you are familiar with. Discuss the details of this business, including the following:

- Its name
- Its location
- The kind of food/products it sells
- Its pricing (expensive or inexpensive)
- Its selling points (how it's different and why people will like it)

Then write a radio advertisement (5–7 sentences) for the business, store, or restaurant you chose. One partner will read your advertisement to the class. Both or all partners should be ready to answer questions from your classmates!

Check Your Progress

1 Fill in the blanks with correct words from the box.

accessory	electronic	get tired of	districts	genuine
fashionable	selection	imported	souvenirs	cuisine

1. The best place to buy ______________ is in Chinatown.
2. It's exciting to wear ______________ clothing and shoes.
3. The farmers' market in San Francisco has a large ______________ of fruits and vegetables.
4. Chinese ______________ is often inexpensive and delicious.
5. There are several good shopping ______________ in San Francisco.
6. I really ______________ the crowds at the beach.
7. I bought a lovely ______________ to wear with my dress.
8. My brothers love to go shopping for ______________ goods such as digital watches and Bluetooth headphones.
9. The furniture is expensive because it is ______________ from America.
10. Do you like the store? I want your ______________ opinion.

2 Listen to the conversation. Circle true or false. Track 095

1. Mr. and Mrs. Chen are in a Chinatown market. true false
2. Chinatown is crowded in the morning. true false
3. The couple is buying fruits, vegetables, and some snacks. true false
4. The couple likes going to Chinatown every weekend. true false
5. Mr. Chen doesn't like shopping in Chinatown. true false

3 Listen again. Circle the correct answers.

1. The Chinese couple (lives / doesn't live) in San Francisco.
2. They like (to go / to leave) to the Chinese market in the morning.
3. Vendors (buy / sell) fruits and snacks in Chinatown.
4. The Chinese market is a great place to (log in / shop around) for fruits, vegetables, and snacks.

4 Fill in the blanks with the correct phrasal verbs from the box.

hang out	miss out (on)	get around	find out	check out

1. You should come to the art gallery this weekend. You don't want to ________________ some great exhibits!
2. The easiest way to ________________ the area is to take a taxi.
3. I like to ________________ the best deals when I go shopping.
4. I will ________________ what time we should meet at the bus stop.
5. My friend wants to ________________ at the beach this Saturday.

8D Let's Take the Subway

A Model Conversation

Read the conversation. Then listen. Track 096

Kevin: We have a few hours before our flight. Why don't we do some shopping? We haven't spent much time in Union Square yet.

Tori: Well, okay, as long as you're sure we have enough time. We still need to pick up our luggage at the hotel and drop the rental car off.

Kevin: Don't worry; there's plenty of time. I need to get some souvenirs for my family. Otherwise, I know they'll be upset with me. Should we drive?

Tori: No, it's almost **rush hour**. Plus, I heard it's really hard to find parking. What about a streetcar?

Kevin: Too slow. Let's take the BART. Here, I found the map online. We can get on at the station across the street and take the yellow **line** to Powell Street. Then, we can walk to Union Square. We don't even need to **transfer**.

Tori: Great. How much is the **fare**?

Kevin: That **depends on** the distance. The ticket machine will **calculate** that for us.

Tori: All right, let's get going. Unless we leave right now, we'll be **stuck** in a crowded train with all the **commuters**!

Brief note

The Bay Area Rapid Transit or "BART" is a light rail public transportation that operates in San Francisco.

B Vocabulary

Read the conversation again. With a partner, match the bold words in the conversation to the correct definitions.

1. ______________ in a difficult situation that is hard to get out of
2. ______________ to find a number using math
3. ______________ is determined by (something)
4. ______________ people traveling to or from work
5. ______________ to change from one bus, train, etc., to another
6. ______________ the time of day when many people are going to or from work
7. ______________ a part of a subway or bus system; a certain train or bus route
8. ______________ the cost of taking a bus, train, etc.

C Vocabulary Comprehension

Look at the map and fill in the blanks in the conversation below. Then listen and check your answers. Track 097

Man: Excuse me. Can I take the subway from the Expo Center to the airport?

Woman: Sure. The ❶ ______________ line goes to Union Station. There, you can ❷ ______________ to the ❸ ______________ line. Then go ❹ ______________ stops to Gateway Station. Transfer to the ❺ ______________ line and go one more stop.

Man: Thanks. What's the ❻ ______________?

Woman: That ❼ ______________ ______________ whether you want a one-way or round-trip ticket.

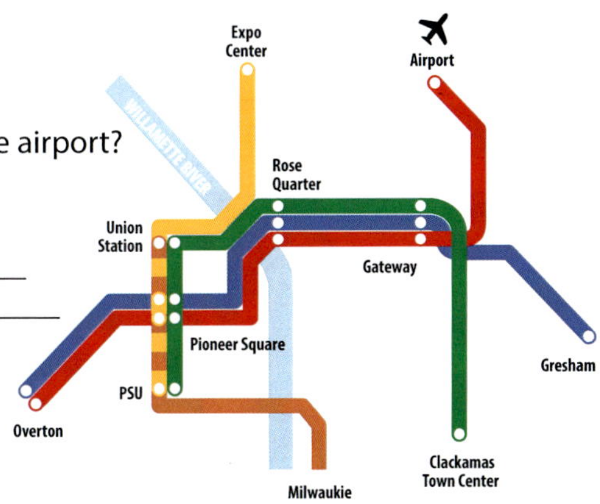

With a partner, practice the conversation. Then take turns choosing two stations on the map and asking your partner for directions from one station to the other.

D Grammar

Ways to express conditions

Brief note

As with other subordinating conjunctions, the two clauses can come in either order.
***As long as** you're sure we have enough time, we can go shopping.*
*We'll be stuck with all the commuters **unless** we leave right now!*

ways to express conditions		
Besides the word *if*, there are several ways to talk about conditions in English.		
expression	**meaning**	**example**
as long as / so long as (conjunctions)	(only) if	We can go shopping **as long as** you're sure we have enough time. (= ... if you're sure we have enough time.)
unless (conjunction)	if not ... then	**Unless** we leave right now, we'll be stuck with all the commuters! (= If we don't leave right now, …)
otherwise (sentence adverb)	if not	I have to get souvenirs for my family. **Otherwise**, they'll be upset. (= ... If not, they'll be upset.)

E Grammar Practice

Fill in the blanks with the correct expressions from above.

1. ____________ we remember to take an umbrella, we should be okay!
2. You should try to leave by four. ____________, you'll get stuck in rush-hour traffic.
3. ____________ the subway is on time, we'll make it to the movie.
4. ____________ you study harder, you won't pass your final exam.
5. You can borrow my car ____________ you return it by midnight.
6. We'll have to cancel the trip ____________ the weather improves.
7. She has to take a taxi, not the bus. ____________, she'll be late.
8. ____________ it all goes smoothly, the show will be a success.

Rewrite the sentences using the given expression.

9. The bus is free if you have a student ID. (as long as)

____

10. If I don't find my keys, I won't be able to give you a ride. (unless)

____

F Use the Language

Subway systems

1. Go online and find a map of a subway, tube, or metro system in another city or country. Describe where it is and give your opinion of it. Does it seem convenient? Does it seem difficult to use? How does it compare to the subway system in your city or country?
2. With a partner, design a subway map for your city or make suggestions to improve your city's subway system. If you could design a whole new subway system to make travel more convenient in your city, what would you do? What would it look like? Draw it and present it to another pair of students. Explain the reasons for your decisions.

Check Your Progress

1 **Listen to the conversation. Put a check mark (✓) next to the sentences you hear.** Track 098

1. ☐ I'm going to have dinner at a restaurant in Manhattan after work.
2. ☐ I don't like going out during rush hour.
3. ☐ The reservation is at 4:00.
4. ☐ I'm still getting used to the subway system.
5. ☐ I think line 2 will be the slowest way to get to Manhattan.
6. ☐ Let's get back to work so we can leave right at 6:00.

2 **Fill in the blanks with the correct words from the box.**

rush hour	line	transfer	fare	stuck	commuters

I was 30 minutes late for work today. First, I woke up late. I usually drive to work, but I was afraid I'd be late because of all the cars during ❶ ________________. So I decided to take the subway. But this wasn't much better. I didn't have money to pay the ❷ ________________ because the ticket machines only take cash. So I had to wait in line at the ticket window. There were also many ❸ ________________ on the train, so the ride was really uncomfortable! Then I made the wrong ❹ ________________ and got on ❺ ________________ 2 instead of 5. I was ❻ ________________ on the wrong train and went two extra stops. What a terrible day!

3 **Circle the correct expressions.**

1. We can go by subway (as long as / unless) there is enough time.
2. I don't like going out during rush hour (so long as / unless) I have the day off from work.
3. You should take the bus to the grocery store. (Unless / Otherwise), you will have to transfer twice on the subway.
4. (As long as / Unless) Jacob charges his phone battery, we won't be able to contact him.

4 **Describe each picture using language from today's class.**

____

____

____

____

____

____

____

____

____

8E At the Mall

A Model Conversation

Brief note

A "fitness tracker" is an electronic device that you wear on the wrist or ankle and that you can connect to your computer or phone. It records information about your physical activity, heart rate, etc.

Read the conversation. Then listen. Track 099

Anna: So, are you done with your shopping?

Eric: Yep, I am, and that's good because I've run out of money. Did you get to see the whole mall? This place is enormous. I'd love it if we had a mall like this back home.

Anna: No, I couldn't. And I knew you would love this place, especially with all the cool electronics stores. That reminds me—I have one more purchase to make. I've been planning to get a fitness tracker for my dad.

Eric: Really? Is he into fitness?

Anna: Well, a month ago his doctor told him to exercise more and lose weight. So he's been taking long walks every day. But he doesn't really enjoy it.

Eric: So you think that if he could see how many steps he's taking, it might encourage him to keep going?

Anna: Exactly. And I think he'd appreciate it. He's like you—he loves all electronic devices. They're like toys for him.

Eric: Okay, then let's hurry and pick one out. I've been keeping an eye on the time, and the mall closes in twenty minutes.

B Vocabulary

Listen to each word or phrase. Then write each word next to the correct definition. Track 100

run out of	enormous	purchase	remind	encourage	appreciate	device	keep an eye on

1. ____________________ something bought
2. ____________________ a machine or piece of equipment designed for a specific purpose
3. ____________________ to use up something so that you no longer have any
4. ____________________ to check regularly; to watch carefully
5. ____________________ to cause someone to remember something
6. ____________________ to be thankful for something and understand its importance or value
7. ____________________ extremely big
8. ____________________ to make someone more likely to do something

C In Your World

Ask a partner the following questions. Discuss the answers and share the most interesting things with another pair of students.

- Do you enjoy shopping for electronic devices? When did you last purchase one? What was it?
- Do you shop at a mall? What is your favorite store there?
- Do you prefer shopping in stores or online? Why?
- If you were very rich, how would your shopping habits change?

D Grammar

Present perfect continuous tense

present perfect continuous	
The present perfect continuous is similar to the present perfect. Both tenses are used to talk about actions that began at some time in the past and are connected to the present. With the present perfect continuous, the focus is on the process. The action is or was ongoing, and either is not finished or has recently finished. This tense has the form *have/has* + *been* + present participle.	
the action has been ongoing and is not finished	I**'ve been planning** to get my dad a fitness tracker. (I still am.) It**'s been raining** since early this morning. (It still is.) They **haven't been keeping** an eye on the time. (They still aren't.) How long **have** you **been living** here? (You still are.)
the action has been ongoing and has recently finished	It's nice to finally sit down. I**'ve been shopping** all day. Her eyes are red. I think she**'s been crying**. You're covered with sweat. **Have** you **been exercising**? The kitchen smells wonderful. Someone**'s been cooking**.

E Grammar Practice

Circle the correct answers. Then read your answers out loud to your partner.

1. (We've / We're) been having a great time on this vacation!
2. He (haven't / hasn't) been learning English for very long.
3. I've been (waiting / wait) for you for the last five hours!
4. Have (been you and Doug / you and Doug been) dating this past year?

Fill in the blanks with the correct forms of the given verbs in the present perfect continuous.

5. I'm healthier because I ______________________ (use) a fitness tracker for a while.
6. He ______________________ (remind) me about his birthday for two weeks!
7. How long ______________________ you ______________________ (work) at the mall?

F Use the Language

Talking about your devices

Interview a partner about technology that they use. It could be a phone, a computer, a tablet, an MP3 player, etc. Ask them 5–10 questions about the device, including where they purchased it, how long they have been using it, and whether they'd recommend that you buy one. When you think you have enough information, write about what your partner said. Do not use the name of the device. Choose another partner, and read your description out loud. Your new partner must try and guess what the device is.

Check Your Progress

1 **Listen and choose the correct answers.** Track 101

1. Tom does not have a ________________.
   a. pencil b. textbook c. notebook
2. The bookstore at the university has ________________ books for Mr. Collins's class.
   a. run out of b. a few c. a lot
3. Tom will have to go to the ________________ to buy the book.
   a. university b. library c. mall
4. Mr. Collins thinks that only ________________ students will do well in his class.
   a. smart b. appreciative c. motivated

2 **Fill in the blanks with the correct forms of the verbs in present perfect continuous tense.**

I have ________________ ________________ (train) for a marathon for three weeks. My coach wants me to run faster, so I ________________ been ________________ (learn) how to keep track of time. Lately, I have ________________ ________________ (do) stretches recommended by my coach. But even with the stretches, my legs ________________ ________________ ________________ (hurt) for a while now. My coach ________________ ________________ ________________ (remind) me to drink lots of water and get enough rest to avoid getting injured.

3 **Match the underlined word in the sentence with the word or phrase with the same meaning.**

1. My mom always comes out to <u>support</u> me at my basketball games. •
2. There was a <u>giant</u> hippo at the zoo. •
3. I really <u>value</u> your opinion about the job. •
4. You should always <u>look after</u> young children. •

- • **a.** keep an eye on
- • **b.** appreciate
- • **c.** enormous
- • **d.** encourage

4 **Complete the sentences.**

1. I (do / don't) enjoy shopping. The reason I (enjoy / don't enjoy) it is ________________________________.
2. When I go shopping at the mall, I usually buy ________________________________.
3. One thing that I have been planning to buy is ________________________________.
4. Online shopping is ________________________________.

8F A New Game

A Model Conversation

Read the conversation. Then listen. Track 102

Brent: Hi. I'm looking for a game, but I don't know the title. I also wanted to pre-order a game and trade in a few, too.

Clerk: No problem. Let's start with the game you're looking for.

Brent: It's a new space shooting game. My brother made me play it with him during the holiday. Then he got me to promise to buy it. Sorry, I'm not much of a gamer.

Clerk: No. It's okay. One second. Here are all the newest shooting games. I think this is the one you're talking about. You can switch from first-person point of view to third-person point of view. You can also customize your character and weapons to your level.

Brent: Yeah, that's the one.

Clerk: What else can I help you with?

Brent: Right, I want to pre-order the new *Call of Duty* game.

Clerk: Okay. Just fill in this form. You also wanted to do a trade-in? Can I see the games? Hmm. Okay, well, I can give you about $30 cash for all of these or $40 of credit.

Brent: I'll take the store credit then.

B Vocabulary

Listen to each word or phrase. Then write each word next to the correct definition. Track 103

pre-order	trade in	space	point of view	customize
character	weapon	level	cash	store credit

1. ______________ to change something to fit your tastes
2. ______________ to buy something by selling something else you own
3. ______________ the position from which something is seen
4. ______________ something (such as a gun, knife, etc.) used to fight, attack, or defend
5. ______________ the area between planets, stars, and galaxies
6. ______________ physical money in the form of bills and coins
7. ______________ money in the form of a document that can only be used in a particular store
8. ______________ a person in a movie, novel, or game
9. ______________ to order an item before it is available for purchase
10. ______________ a way to show one's rank, experience, or qualifications

C In Your World

Do you like to play video games? Why or why not? Who do you know that likes to play video games? Do you think playing video games is a good thing? Why or why not? Discuss with a partner and then with the class.

D Grammar

Causative verbs

causative verbs	
The verbs *make*, *get*, and *have* can be used as causative verbs. This means you use them to talk about causing someone to do something, or causing something to happen. Causative verb phrases have the form *make/have* + object + base verb, or *get* + object + infinitive.	
make/have + object + base verb	My brother **made me play** that game. (I didn't want to play it, but my brother caused me to play it.) I'**ll have the salesperson show** me something else. (I'll ask the salesperson to show me something else.)
get + object + infinitive	To **get the characters to switch** point of view, press here. (You can cause the characters to switch point of view by pressing here.)

Brief note

Make is the strongest in meaning; it usually means someone was given an order. *Have* can be used for an order or polite request. *Get* often means that a person was persuaded (talked into) doing something. It's also used for non-human objects: *I can't get my hair to stay straight.*

E Grammar Practice

Underline the error and rewrite each sentence correctly.

1. He made me to wash my hands again. ________________
2. I can't get my daughter go to sleep! ________________
3. Can you get the car starting? ________________
4. I'll has the delivery guy leave it at the door. ________________
5. Can you have her to call me when she comes in? ________________
6. My teacher makes us to practice new words every day. ________________
7. I got my brother cleaned my room the other day. ________________
8. She always makes us to feel bad about not calling her. ________________

F Use the Language

Writing a formal email

You recently purchased a game application for your phone. You thought all the in-game items were free, but you were charged for them unexpectedly. Write a short formal email to the company asking for an explanation and refund.

New Message

To CC Bcc

Subject

Dear Access Games,

Send

Now share your email with a partner. Write a response to your partner's email.

Check Your Progress

1 Read the conversation. Fill in blanks with the correct words from the box. Then listen and check. Track 104

characters	trade in	cash	point of view	pre-order

Clerk: Hello. How can I assist you today?

Jesse: I would like to ____________________ a game.

Clerk: I can help you with that.

Jesse: Great. I want that new shooting game—the one with all strange ____________________, such as the giant gorilla and the robot.

Clerk: Is it in first-person ____________________? Hmm. I think this is the one you're talking about.

Jesse: Yeah. That's it. Also, can I ____________________ a game for a discount?

Clerk: We can't give any discounts on games that haven't been released yet.

Jesse: Okay, then I will just pay for the pre-order. Do I have to pay the total price now?

Clerk: No, you can pre-order with just $10. We accept credit cards, or you can pay in ____________________.

Jesse: I will be using my credit card. Thank you.

2 Underline the errors and rewrite the sentences correctly.

1. He have to buy the new video game online because it is not available at the store.

   ____

2. It is important that you got to the electronic store before it closes.

   ____

3. The mall will be closed for the holiday, so people will has to shop early.

   ____

4. To got to the next level, you need to finish this mission first.

   ____

3 Read the email and circle true or false.

Dear Game Clerk,

I was in your store a few weeks ago. I pre-ordered the new Galactic Battle series game. I was emailing you to find out if the game has arrived yet. On the receipt, it states the game will arrive in the store in two weeks. It's been two weeks, and I haven't received any new messages about my order. If you could email me back, I would greatly appreciate it.

Thank you,
Jesse Smith

1. Jesse was in the store last night. true false
2. He wants to know when his game will arrive. true false
3. The game was pre-ordered. true false
4. He bought the new Galactic Battle series game. true false
5. He expected the game to arrive one week ago. true false

8G Stay Safe

A Authentic Text: Safety poster

Read the safety poster.

Brief note

"Black Friday" is the biggest shopping day of the year in the US. It marks the start of holiday shopping, and it takes place after the Thanksgiving Day holiday.

This year's Black Friday Sale will start at 9 a.m. For your safety, please read the following tips:

1. Watch your surroundings. Last year's sale brought in a record number of shoppers. Be aware and cautious while shopping.
2. Do not leave your belongings unattended. Lost items can be collected at the Lost & Found. But the mall is not responsible for stolen items.
3. Keep your money, wallet, and other valuables in a safe place.
4. Know where your nearest exit is. In case of emergency, calmly proceed to the exit.
5. For tourists, the duty-free exchange is located on the 2nd floor. Please bring all your receipts and items after shopping to collect your tax refund.

Thank you for shopping at Sheffield Mall. We wish you safe and happy holidays.

B Vocabulary

Match each word with the correct definition.

1. aware •	• **a.** to go and get; to pick up
2. cautious •	• **b.** an important or expensive item that someone owns
3. belongings •	• **c.** a place where things are traded
4. collect •	• **d.** careful; avoiding danger
5. receipt •	• **e.** to move in a specific direction
6. valuable •	• **f.** not taxed when taken out of the country
7. emergency •	• **g.** things a person owns
8. proceed •	• **h.** a paper that shows what was purchased
9. exchange •	• **i.** paying attention to what is happening around you
10. duty-free •	• **j.** an unexpected problem or dangerous situation

C In Your World

With a partner, make a list of safety tips for people visiting your city. Share your list with another pair of students. Then show it to your teacher.

D Grammar

Leaving out articles for brevity

<table>
<tr><th colspan="2">leaving out articles for brevity</th></tr>
<tr><td colspan="2">Sometimes, there is a need to leave out articles (a, an, the) to make sentences short and easy to read. On signs and posters, articles are often left out to make room for more important information.
Articles are also left out in news headlines to make room for more words on the page.</td></tr>
<tr><td>Do not use <s>the</s> elevator. → Do not use elevator.</td><td>Proceed to <s>the</s> nearest exit. → Proceed to nearest exit.</td></tr>
<tr><td colspan="2"><s>A</s> local man finds <s>a</s> wallet with $1,000. → Local Man Finds Wallet with $1,000
<s>The</s> city announces <s>a</s> new football stadium. → City Announces New Football Stadium</td></tr>
</table>

E Grammar Practice

Read the safety instructions for a new laptop. Rewrite the instructions, adding articles where they have been removed.

1. Shut down laptop when not using it.

   ____

2. Turn off computer before placing into carrying bag.

   ____

3. Do not put computer directly on legs. It can burn skin. Use table or other hard surface.

   ____

4. Check fan frequently to avoid overheating.

   ____

5. Clean air vents regularly, and never put anything into air vents.

   ____

6. Do not try to clean inside of computer screen.

   ____

F Quick Review

Look back at the brief notes in this unit.

1. What is another word for *economy class*? ______________________
2. What device measures your heart rate and physical activity? ______________________
3. Which of the following is correct, *pick it up* or *pick up it?* ______________________

G Use the Language

Emergency poster

1. With a partner, think of an emergency situation. Design an emergency poster for it. Be sure to include specific instructions on what to do. Make the poster as clear and concise as possible. Include images and colors that are appropriate. Go online and look at some examples to help you. Make the poster and present it to the class.
2. When you are finished, imagine that an emergency like the one described in your poster has actually happened. Write a short news article about the emergency. Include a catchy headline. Present your article to the class.

Check Your Progress

1 Find and circle the words.

D	U	T	Y	F	R	E	E	Y	M	C	G
T	Q	T	V	E	Y	Y	C	Q	A	L	T
P	S	W	Y	L	G	N	K	U	T	C	P
I	M	G	L	V	E	N	T	W	E	Q	M
E	P	M	N	G	A	I	A	L	N	J	G
C	N	R	R	I	O	L	L	H	B	W	M
E	R	E	O	U	G	O	U	Y	C	T	T
R	M	R	S	C	C	N	W	A	V	X	R
E	R	A	W	A	E	R	O	N	B	Z	E
M	D	M	X	J	R	E	Y	L	T	L	J
N	W	Z	W	Y	D	L	D	Z	E	B	E
T	T	B	V	T	R	T	R	D	Z	B	G

receipt	proceed
valuable	aware
belongings	cautious
duty-free	exchange
emergency	collect

2 Read the text and circle true or false.

When people visit the local markets in Thailand, they are surprised to see that there are a lot of people shopping. So, it's important for travelers to be aware of their surroundings to stay safe. One tip is to not carry too much money or other valuables while looking around. Sometimes travelers aren't cautious while they shop. They can easily lose their belongings or get things stolen. It's always wise to keep an eye on your things while shopping in the markets. The best way to have a great shopping experience is to prepare wisely before traveling.

1. In Thailand, there aren't a lot of people in the markets. true false
2. People should carry a lot of money while shopping. true false
3. Sometimes travelers aren't cautious while shopping. true false
4. Travelers' belongings are easily stolen. true false
5. It's best to prepare wisely before traveling. true false

3 Rewrite the statements without the articles.

1. Buy a ticket before getting on the train. ____________________.
2. Take found items to the lost-and-found. ____________________.
3. In case of a fire, please go to the nearest exit. ____________________.
4. To return items, bring the receipts to the customer service desk.

____________________.

4 Write questions for the answers.

1. ____________________?

I would call the police in an emergency.

2. ____________________?

The fire department will show up to put out dangerous fires.

3. ____________________?

You should check the lost-and-found at the mall.

4. ____________________?

If there is an emergency at the mall, try to find the nearest exit.

Unit Review

A Welcome to New York!

Read the tourist information poster. With a partner, fill in the blanks with the correct words and phrases from the box.

districts	fashionable	genuine	fare	purchase	keep an eye on
aware	cautious	get	emergency	street vendors	as long as

Welcome to New York: Tips for Tourists

People come from around the world to visit New York City. ________________ ________________ ________________ you are ________________, you will have a safe and enjoyable time here.

Stay Safe!

- ★ The subway is a great way to get around. But always ________________ ________________ ________________ ________________ your belongings, especially on crowded trains.
- ★ In subway and train stations, people may try to ________________ you to give them the ________________ for a ticket home. This is a common scam.
- ★ For your safety, be ________________ of your transportation options at all times. Always find out where the nearest subway station is, so that you can catch a train quickly in an ________________.

Shop Smart!

- ★ Fifth Avenue, with its ________________ department stores, is the most famous shopping street in New York. But be sure to check out Canal Street and Chinatown, too. Locals appreciate these areas for their interesting smaller shops.
- ★ There are many ________________ ________________ in busy shopping ________________ Some will tell you they're selling real brand-name clothes, shoes, and accessories, but the items may not be ________________. If the price seems too good to be true, you should probably ________________ the item in a store instead.

B Create a Poster

In a small group, create a similar poster about your city (or another city you all know well). Include tips about getting around, safety, shopping, and any other important information for visitors. Present your poster to the class.

C Reminder

Put a check mark (✓) next to the things you can do.

_____ Understand instructions expressed in simple language (for example, how to use public telephones or ticket machines, safety information, or directions)

_____ Write a short, formal email asking for or giving simple information

_____ Write simple texts about experiences or events (for example, describing your feelings and reactions about a trip)

Further Practice

A Warm Up

With a partner, put the words and phrases from the box into the correct categories. Some words can be put in more than one category.

turn on log in	transfer device	character cash	rush hour exchange	receipt commuter

Transportation	Shopping	Electronics/Games

B Brainstorm

You and your partner have just arrived at your favorite shopping mall. Discuss ideas for spending the day there. Consider what you will do, what you'd like to buy or need to buy, where you will eat, and how you will fill the day. You need to stay at the mall from the morning to the evening.

C Role-play

Now, using your ideas from part B, create a detailed plan for the day with your partner and write a conversation. Perform your conversation for the class.

Plan

1. ______________________
____

2. ______________________
____

3. ______________________
____

4. ______________________
____

Conversation

A: ______________________

B: ______________________

A: ______________________

B: ______________________

A: ______________________

B: ______________________

A: ______________________

B: ______________________

MEMO

MEMO

MEMO

MEMO